A Comparative Study of the Literatures of Egypt, Palestine, and Mesopotamia

The Ancient Near East: Classic Studies

K. C. Hanson
Series Editor

Albert T. Clay
*Light on the Old Testament
from Babel*

Albert T. Clay
*The Origin of
Biblical Tradition*

Leonard W. King
*Legends of Babylon and Egypt
in Relation to
Hebrew Tradition*

Friedrich Delitzsch
Babel and Bible

George Smith
Assyrian Discoveries

George Smith & A. H. Sayce
*The Chaldean Account
of Genesis*

T. Eric Peet
*A Comparative Study
of the Literatures of
Egypt, Palestine, and
Mesopotamia*

A Comparative Study of the Literatures of Egypt, Palestine, and Mesopotamia

Egypt's Contribution to
the Literature of the
Ancient World

T. Eric Peet

New Foreword and Bibliography by
K. C. Hanson

Wipf & Stock
PUBLISHERS
Eugene, Oregon

A COMPARATIVE STUDY OF THE LITERATURES OF EGYPT,
PALESTINE, AND MESOPOTAMIA
Egypt's Contribution to the Literature of the Ancient World

The Ancient Near East: Classic Studies

ISBN 13: 978-1-59752-739-2

Cataloging-in-Publication data

Peet, T. Eric (Thomas Eric), 1882–1934.
 A comparative study of the literatures of Egypt, Palestine, and
 Mesopotamia : Egypt's contribution to the literature of the ancient
 world / T. Eric Peet. New foreword and bibliography by K. C.
 Hanson

 The Ancient Near East: Classic Studies

 Note: The Schweich Lectures of the British Academy ; 1929

 ISBN 13: 978-1-59752-739-2

 xx + 136 p.; cm.

 1. Egyptian literature—History and criticism. 2. Egyptian literature—
 Relation to the Old Testament. 3. Literature, comparative—Hebrew
 and Egyptian. 4. Literature, comparative—Egyptian and Assyro-
 Babylonian. 5. Literature, comparative—Assyro-Babylonian and
 Egyptian. 6. Literature, Ancient. I. Hanson, K. C. (Kenneth C.). II.
 British Academy. III. Title. IV. Series.

 PJ1488 .P4 2007

Contents

Series Foreword

The archaeological discoveries of ancient cities and texts in Mesopotamia, Egypt, and Syria-Palestine began in earnest in the nineteenth century and only accelerated in the twentieth and twenty-first
centuries. A few of the most significant early explorations and excavations make the point:

- In 1838, Robinson explored and inaugurated the geographical
  study of Palestine, especially exploring Jerusalem, including
  Hezekiah's Tunnel.[1]

- Funded by King Friedrich Wilhelm IV of Prussia, Richard
  Lepsius discovered several monuments from the Old
  Kingdom of Egypt during his three-year expedition (1843–
  1845).[2]

- The earliest treasures of Assyria were excavated by Layard
  at Calah (Nimrud) and Botta at Nineveh (the Kuyunjik
  mound in Mosul) in the 1840s.[3]

- Sir W. K. Loftus carried out the earliest explorations of
  Ur (Tell Muqqayyar) in 1849. But it was Sir C. Leonard
  Wooley who did the systematic excavations (1922–34).[4]

- Charles Warren surveyed the topography of Jerusalem and
  the temple mount in 1867 and 1870.

---

1. Edward Robinson and Eli Smith, *Biblical Researches in Palestine and in the Adjacent Regions: A Journal of Travels in the Year 1838,* 3 vols. (Boston: Crocker & Brewster, 1841).

2. C. R. Lepsius, *Denkmäler aus Aegypten und Aethiopien,* 12 vols. (Berlin: Nicolaische Buchhandlung, 1849–56).

3. Austen Henry Layard, *Nineveh and Its Remains,* 2 vols. (New York: Putnam, 1849); idem, *Discoveries in the Ruins of Nineveh and Babylon* (New York: Harper, 1853); Paul Émile Botta, *Monument de Ninive* (Paris: Imprimerie Nationale, 1849–50).

4. C. L. Wooley, *Ur Excavations,* 10 vols. (London: Oxford University Press, 1927–74).

- The ancient Egyptian sites of Tanis and Gizeh were explored by Sir Flinders Petrie in the 1880s.[5]

- The University of Pennsylvania began excavations of Nippur (southeast of Baghdad) in 1889.[6]

- Under the auspices of the Deutsche Orient-Gesellschaft (German Orient Association), Koldewey excavated Babylon (part of modern Baghdad) from 1899 to 1918.[7]

The remains of ancient societies often require decades to unearth, but much longer to interpret and understand. The methods of archaeology have progressed dramatically in recent years. Archaeologists have continuously refined their tools, methods, and techniques. Today archaeology is characterized by pottery identification, classification, and cataloging; disciplined excavation of "squares"; use of sophisticated electronics, such as GPS, infrared, and computer-aided design; and the integration of multiple methodologies, such as epigraphy, art history, physical anthropology, paleobotany, and climatology.

The interpretation of ancient Near Eastern history and cultures has also progressed. An increasing number of documents has been unearthed. The vast document collections from Tel el-Amarna, Nippur, Mari, Nuzi, Ebla, Ugarit, and the Dead Sea caves are just some of the more spectacular examples. These provide an enormous amount of detail about the royal administrations, business transactions, land tenure systems, taxes, political propaganda, mythologies, marriage practices, and much more. And things that sometimes seem unique about one culture at first look often fit into larger patterns of relationship when the surrounding cultures are better understood.

The Ancient Near East: Classic Studies (**ANECS**) reprints classic works that have brought the results of archaeology, textual, and historical investigations to audiences of scholars, students, and the general public. While the discussions continue and the results

5. W. M. Flinders Petrie, *Tanis,* 2 vols. (Egypt Exploration Fund, 1880–1888); idem, *The Pyramids and Temples of Gizeh* (London: Field & Tuer, 1883).

6. Clarence S. Fisher, *Excavations at Nippur* (Philadelphia: Babylonian Expedition of the University of Pennsylvania, 1905).

7. Robert Koldewey, *The Excavations at Babylon,* trans. Agnes S. Johns (London: Macmillan, 1914).

of earlier investigations are continuously re-examined, these classic works remain of interest and importance.

—K. C. Hanson
Series Editor

Foreword

T. Eric Peet was an English archaeologist and Egyptologist. He was the Brunner Professor of Egyptology at the University of Liverpool. He had previously been the Laycock Student in Egyptology at Worcester College, Oxford University. He co-directed the excavations at both Abydos and Amarna for the Egypt Exploration Society. The present volume is based upon his Schweich Lectures of the British Academy for 1929.

In addition to the present work, Peet's publications include the following:

The Stone and Bronze Ages in Italy and Sicily. Oxford: Clarendon, 1909.

Contributions to the Study of the Prehistoric Period of Malta. London: British School of Rome, 1910.

Rough Stone Monuments and Their Builders. Harper's Library of Living Thought. London: Harper, 1912.

With Edouard Naville et al. *The Cemeteries of Abydos.* 3 vols. London: Egypt Exploration Fund, 1913–14.

The Stela of Sebek-khu: The Earliest Record of an Egyptian Campaign in Asia. Manchester: Sherratt & Hughes, 1914.

"The Art of Predynastic Period." *Journal of Egyptian Archaeology* 2 (1915) 88–94.

"The Great Tomb Robberies of the Ramesside Age. Papyri Mayer A & B." *Journal of Egyptian Archaeology* 2 (1915) 173–77.

With Alan H. Gardiner. *The Inscriptions of Sinai.* London: Egypt Exploration Fund, 1917.

The Mayer Papyri A & B. London: Egypt Exploration Fund, 1920.

"Excavations at Tell el-Amarna: A Preliminary Report." *Journal of Egyptian Archaeology* 7 (1921) 169–85.

Egypt and the Old Testament. The Ancient World. Liverpool: University Press of Liverpool, 1922.

"Arithmetic in the Middle Kingdom." *Journal of Egyptian Archaeology* 9 (1923) 91–95.

With C. Leonard Woolley. *The City of Akhenaten.* 3 parts in 2 vols. London: Egypt Exploration Fund, 1923.

The Rhind Mathematical Papyrus: British Museum 10057 and 10058. Liverpool: University Press of Liverpool, 1923.

"A Historical Document of the Ramesside Age." *Journal of Egyptian Archaeology* 10 (1924).

"Fresh Light on the Tomb-Robberies of the Twentieth Dynasty at Thebes: Some New Papyri in London and Turin." *Journal of Egyptian Archaeology* 11 (1925) 37–55.

"The Supposed Revolution of the High Priest Amenhotep under Ramesses IX." *Journal of Egyptian Archaeology* 12 (1926) 254–59.

With Jaroslav Cerny. "A Marriage Settlement of the Twentieth Dynasty." *Journal of Egyptian Archaeology* 13 (1927) 30– 39.

"A. G. K. Hayter." *Journal of Egyptian Archaeology* 14 (1928) 323–24.

"The Chronological Problems of the Twentieth Dynasty." *Journal of Egyptian Archaeology* 14 (1928) 52–73.

With Guiseppe Botti. *Il Giornale della Necropoli de Tebe.* Torino: Bocca, 1928.

The Great Tomb-Robberies of the Twentieth Egyptian Dynasty. 2 vols. Oxford: Clarendon, 1930.

"Mathematics in Ancient Egypt." *Bulletin of the John Rylands Library* 15 (1931) 409–41.

"A Problem in Egyptian Geometry." *Journal of Egyptian Archaeology* 17 (1931) 100–106.

"The Egyptian Words for 'Money,' 'Buy,' and 'Sell.'" In *Studies Presented to F. Ll. Griffith,* edited by S. R. K. Glanville, 122–27. London: Oxford University Press, 1932.

The Present Position of Egyptological Studies: An Inaugural Lecture Delivered before the University of Oxford on 17 January 1934. Oxford: Clarendon, 1934.

—K. C. Hanson

Bibliography

Alster, Bendt. "Epic Tales from Ancient Sumer: Enmerkar, Lugalbanda, and Other Cunning Heroes." In *Civilization of the Ancient Near East,* edited by Jack M. Sasson, 4:2315–26. New York: Scribner, 1995.

Batto, Bernard F. *Slaying the Dragon: Mythmaking in the Biblical Tradition.* Louisville: Westminster John Knox, 1992.

Beyerlin, Walter, editor. *Near Eastern Religious Texts Relating to the Old Testament.* Translated by John Bowden. Old Testament Library. Philadelphia: Westminster, 1978.

Blackman, Aylward M. *The Ancient Egyptians: A Sourcebook of Their Writings.* New York: Harper & Row, 1966.

Chavalas, Mark W., and K. Lawson Younger, editors. *Mesopotamia and the Bible: Comparative Explorations.* Grand Rapids: Baker Academic, 2002.

Clark, R. T. *Myth and Symbol in Ancient Egypt.* New York: Grove, 1959.

Clay, Albert T. *Light on the Old Testament from Babel.* 1907. Reprinted, The Ancient Near East: Classic Studies. Eugene, Ore.: Wipf & Stock, 2006.

———. *The Origin of Biblical Traditions.* 1923. Reprinted, The Ancient Near East: Classic Studies. Eugene, Ore.: Wipf & Stock, 2006.

Coogan, Michael D. *Stories from Ancient Canaan.* Philadelphia: Westminster, 1978.

Dalley, Stephanie. *Myths from Mesopotamia.* Oxford: Oxford Univ. Press, 1989.

Delitzsch, Friedrich. *Das babylonische Weltschöpfungsepos.* Abhandlungen der sächsischen Gesellschaft der Wissenschaften zu Leipzig 17. Leipzig: Hirzel, 1896.

———. *Babel and Bibel.* 1902. Reprinted, The Ancient Near East: Classic Studies. Eugene, Ore.: Wipf & Stock, 2006.

Dijk, Jacobus van. "Myth and Mythmaking in Ancient Egypt." In *Civilization of the Ancient Near East,* edited by Jack M. Sasson, 3:1697–710. New York: Scribner, 1995.

Fisher, Loren R., editor. *Ras Shamra Parallels: The Texts from Ugarit and the Hebrew Bible.* Vols. 1–2. Analecta Orientalia 49, 50. Rome: Pontifical Biblical Institute Press, 1972, 1975.

Foster, Benjamin R. *Before the Muses: An Anthology of Akkadian Literature.* 3d ed. Bethesda, Md.: CDL, 2005.

———. *From Distant Days: Myths, Tales and Poetry from Ancient Mesopotamia.* Bethesda, MD: CDL, 1995.

———, Douglas Frayne, and Gary Beckman. *The Epic of Gilgamesh: A New Translation, Analogues, Criticism.* Norton Critical Edition. New York: Norton, 2001.

Fox, Michael V. *The Song of Songs and Ancient Egyptian Love Songs.* Madison: University of Wisconsin Press, 1985.

Frankfort, Henri. *The Problem of Similarity in Ancient Near Eastern Religions.* Oxford: Clarendon, 1951.

Gaster, T. H. *Thespis: Ritual, Myth and Drama in the Ancient Near East.* Rev. ed. Garden City, NY: Doubleday, 1961.

George, A. R. *The Babylonian Gilgamesh Epic: Introduction, Critical Edition, and Cuneiform Texts.* 2 vols. Oxford: Oxford Univ. Press, 2003.

Gibson, J. C. L. *Canaanite Myths and Legends.* 2d ed. Old Testament Studies 3. Edinburgh: T. & T. Clark, 1977.

Gordon, Cyrus H. "Poetic Legends and Myths from Ugarit." *Berytus* 25 (1977) 5–133.

———, and Gary A. Rendsburg. *The Bible and the Ancient Near East.* 4th ed. New York: Norton, 1998.

Görg, Manfred. *Gott–König–Reden in Israel und Ägypten.* Beträge zur Wissenschaft vom Alten und Neuen Testament 6/5. Stuttgart: Kohlhammer, 1975.

Gunkel, Hermann. *Genesis.* Translated by Mark E. Biddle. Mercer Library of Biblical Studies. Macon, GA: Mercer University Press, 1997.

———. *Creation and Chaos in the Primeval Era and the Eschaton: Religio-Historical Study of Genesis 1 and Revelation 12.* Translated by K. William Whitney Jr. Biblical Resources Series. Grand Rapids: Eerdmans, 2006.

Hallo, William W., and K. Lawson Younger Jr., editors. *The Context of Scripture.* Vol. 1: *Canonical Compositions from the Biblical World.* Leiden: Brill, 1997.

Heidel, Alexander. *The Gilgamesh Epic and Old Testament Parallels.* 2d ed. Chicago: University of Chicago Press, 1949.

———. *The Babylonian Genesis.* 2d ed. Chicago: University of Chicago Press, 1951.

Hess, Richard S., and David Toshio Tsumura, editors. *I Studied Inscriptions from before the Flood: Ancient Near Eastern, Literary, and Linguistic Approaches to Genesis 1–11.* Sources for Biblical and Theological Study 4. Winona Lake, IN: Eisenbrauns, 1994.

Hollis, Susan Tower. "Tales of Magic and Wonder from Ancient Egypt." In *Civilization of the Ancient Near East,* edited by Jack M. Sasson, 4:2255–64. New York: Scribner, 1995.

Hooke, S. H. *Middle Eastern Mythology.* Baltimore: Penguin, 1963.

Irvin, Dorothy. *Mytharion: The Comparison of Tales from the Old Testament and the Ancient Near East.* Alter Orient und Altes Testament 32. Neukirchen-Vluyn: Neukirchener, 1978.

Jeremias, Alfred. *The Old Testament in the Light of the Ancient East.* 2 vols. Translated by C. L. Beaumont. Edited by C. H. W. Johns. Theological Translation Library 28–29. New York: Putnam, 1911.

Johnston, Philip S. "Death in Egypt and Israel: A Theological Reflection." In *The Old Testament in Its World,* edited by Robert P. Gordon and Johannes C. de Moor, 94–116. Leiden: Brill, 2005.

Kitchen, K. A. *On the Reliability of the Old Testament.* Grand Rapids: Eerdmans, 2003.

Knoppers, Gary N., and Antoine Hirsch, editors. *Egypt, Israel, and the Ancient Mediterranean World: Studies in Honor of Donald B. Redford.* Probleme der Ägyptologie 20. Leiden: Brill, 2004.

Lambert, W. G. "Myth and Mythmaking in Sumer and Akkad." In *Civilization of the Ancient Near East,* edited by Jack M. Sasson, 3:1825–36. New York: Scribner, 1995.

Lange, Armin et al., editors. *Mythos im Alten Testament und Seiner Umwelt: Festschrift für Hans-Peter Müller zum 65. Geburtstag.* Beihefte zur Zeitschrift für die alttestamentliche Wissenschaft 278. Berlin: de Gruyter, 1999.

Lichtheim, Miriam. *Ancient Egyptian Literature.* 3 vols. Berkeley: University of California Press, 1973–.

Lubetski, Meir et al., editors. *Boundaries of the Ancient Near Eastern World: A Tribute to Cyrus H. Gordon.* Journal for the Study of the Old Testament Supplement Series 273. Sheffield: Sheffield Academic, 1998.

Moor, Johannes C. de. *An Anthology of Religious Texts from Ugarit.* Nisaba 16. Leiden: Brill, 1987.

———, and Klaas Spronk. *A Cuneiform Anthology of Religious Texts from Ugarit.* Semitic Study Series 6. Leiden: Brill, 1987.

Moran, William L. *The Amarna Letters.* Baltimore: Johns Hopkins University Press, 1992.

———. "The Gilgamesh Epic: A Masterpiece from Ancient Mesopotamia." In *Civilization of the Ancient Near East,* edited by Jack M. Sasson, 4:2327–36. New York: Scribner, 1995.

Otzen, Benedikt et al. *Myths in the Old Testament.* London: SCM, 1980.

Parker, Simon B., editor. *Ugaritic Narrative Poetry.* Writings from the Ancient World 9. Atlanta: Scholars, 1997.

Pritchard, James B., editor. *Ancient Near Eastern Texts Relating to the Old Testament.* 3d ed. Princeton: Princeton Univ. Press, 1969.

Redford, Donald B. *Egypt, Canaan, and Israel in Ancient Times.* Princeton: Princeton University Press, 1992.

Rogers, Robert William. *Cuneiform Parallels to the Old Testament.* 2d ed.

1926. Reprinted, Ancient Texts and Translations. Eugene, OR: Wipf & Stock, 2005.

Rogerson, John W. *Myth in Old Testament Interpretation.* Beihefte zur Zeitschrift für die alttestamentliche Wissenschaft 134. Berlin: de Gruyter, 1974.

Rummel, Stan, editor. *Ras Shamra Parallels: The Texts from Ugarit and the Hebrew Bible.* Vol. 3. Analecta Orientalia 51. Rome: Pontifical Biblical Institute Press, 1981.

Sayce, A. H. *Lectures on the Origin and Growth of Religion as Illustrated by the Religion of the Ancient Babylonians.* Hibbert Lectures 1887. 5th ed. London: Williams and Norgate, 1898.

———. *The Religions of Ancient Egypt and Babylonia.* Gifford Lectures. Edinburgh: T. & T. Clark, 1902.

Simpson, William Kelly, editor. *The Literature of Ancient Egypt: An Anthology of Stories, Instructions, and Poetry.* New Haven: Yale University Press, 1972.

Smith, George, and A. H. Sayce. *The Chaldean Account of Genesis.* 1876. Reprinted, The Ancient Near East: Classic Studies. Eugene, OR: Wipf & Stock, 2006.

Smith, Mark S. "Myth and Mythmaking in Canaan and Ancient Israel." In *Civilization of the Ancient Near East,* edited by Jack M. Sasson, 3:2031–42. New York: Scribner, 1995.

Thomas, D. Winton, editor. *Documents from Old Testament Times.* 1958. Reprinted, Ancient Texts and Translations. Eugene, OR: Wipf & Stock, 2005.

Washington, Harold C. *Wealth and Poverty in the Instruction of Amenemope and the Hebrew Proverbs.* Society of Biblical Literature Dissertation Series 142. Atlanta: Scholars, 1994.

Wyatt, Nicolas. *Religious Texts from Ugarit: The Words of Ilumilku and His Colleagues.* 2d ed. Biblical Seminar 53. Sheffield: Sheffield Academic, 2002.

Preface

It is seldom easy to find for a course of lectures a title which shall be a perfect description of their contents. In the present case the title chosen is in one sense too wide and in another sense too narrow. It is too wide, partly because in my comparative study I have almost completely avoided any literary analysis of the Hebrew writings, assuming in my readers a knowledge of this subject sufficient to enable them to follow my argument; partly because, being an Egyptologist, I have naturally devoted more consideration to the literature of Egypt than to that of Babylonia. It is too narrow, because, in addition to comparing the literature of Egypt with that of the Hebrews, I have also attempted to assess its absolute value for the world in general and for all time. I shall be happy if my readers will attribute these inconsistencies rather to the difficulty of finding a succinct title than to a habit of irrelevancy.

In the matter of translations from the Egyptian I have invariably worked from the original text, except in one case where this was not yet available; it is hardly necessary to add that in all cases I am heavily indebted to the earlier renderings of my colleagues. While keeping as closely as possible to the originals, I have tried to avoid the bald, stilted translations which have done so much harm to the credit of Egyptian literature. At the same time I realize only too well that had my powers of writing good English been greater I could have made out a still better case for the Egyptians than I have.

In translations from the Babylonian, Sumerian, and Assyrian I have been entirely in the hands of the Semitic and Sumerian scholars. I have, however, taken care that in each case the authorities whose translations I adopted should be the best.

To two workers in the field of Egyptian art and literature I am under special obligations: to Max Pieper, who was the first, so far as I know, to publish an appreciation of Egyptian literature as a whole (see p. 15, note 1); and to Heinrich Schäfer, whose writings on Egyptian art have for the first time shown precisely what is its place in the history of art in general, and what is the nature of the gulf which divides it from Greek art of the classical period. Schäfer's treatment of this last problem led me to put a similar question in the domain of literature; the attempt to answer it has developed into the present lectures.

T. Eric Peet

Note.—In the translations, which are given in italics throughout, square brackets [ ] indicate words which are lost in the original, pointed brackets < > words which the scribe has accidentally omitted, round brackets ( ) words which, though understood in the original, need to be expressed in the translation. The use of these disfiguring signs has been reduced to the minimum.

Two abbreviations are constantly used in the footnotes. Weber, *Lit.* stands for Otto Weber, *Die Literatur der Babylonier und Assyrier* (Der Alter Orient, Ergänzungsband ii), Leipzig, 1907; and Meissner, *Lit.* for Bruno Meissner, *Die Babylonisch-Assyrische Literatur* (Handbuch der Literaturwissenschaft), Wildpark-Potsdam, 1927.

LECTURE I

THE contents of the Old Testament form in many respects the most remarkable body of literature which has come down to us from pre-Christian times. Until quite recently, indeed, they formed the only literature which had survived to bear witness to the great civilizations of the Nearer East; that of Egypt and of Mesopotamia was still a closed book, or indeed a book whose existence was barely suspected. Had it been proposed fifty years ago to make a comparative study of the Old Testament, the literatures chosen for comparison must have been the Greek and the Latin. On grounds of absolute dating there would have been nothing absurd in this, for it was even then known that some of the Hebrew books were no older than much of the literature of Greece or even Rome. At the same time, since the Old Testament was thought to be in the main of very much higher date, the comparison would have commended itself but little to scholars. This feeling is even now not extinct, and it may be good for us sometimes to remind ourselves that little in the Old Testament is more than a century or two earlier than the Homeric poems, that Herodotus was contemporary with Malachi and Obadiah, and that Theocritus was singing in Sicily while the Song of Songs was being compiled in Palestine. No doubt there are considerations which make a comparison between the literatures of the Hebrews and the Greeks somewhat unfruitful, but the question of date is surely not one of them.

During the last hundred years scholarship has revealed the existence of two other eastern literatures which are not only as old as that of the Hebrews but very much older, namely those of Egypt and Babylonia. There seems to be a fair measure of agreement among thoughtful and properly equipped students of the Old Testament that there is little in it, save a few fragments of poetry, which took its present form earlier than about 850 B.C. The literatures of Egypt

B

and Babylonia were at that date already hundreds, one might almost say thousands, of years old. Although much of Babylonian literature is known to us mainly from the Assyrian versions found in Assurbanipal's library, recent discoveries have shown that many of its best epic and lyric productions go back at least two thousand years further, and have their roots in the Sumerian civilization. In Egypt, too, religious literature is found in a highly developed state as early as the Pyramid Texts, which, in the form in which we have them, are as old as 2500 B. C., and possibly go back in part to much earlier originals. Recently, too, good reason has been given for believing that at least two texts of religious import, set in dramatic form, can be traced back to the beginnings of the dynastic period.[1] It is possible that the greatest period of Egyptian literature, as of every other art, is to be placed in the Old Kingdom, the IVth to VIth Dynasties, 2800 to 2200 B. C., and it is quite certain that in the Middle Kingdom, which began in 2000 B. C., most of the literary forms had reached their highest development. And yet this is a whole millennium before the composition of the Pentateuch was begun.

These discoveries make it no longer possible to regard the literature of the Hebrews as an isolated phenomenon in the ancient East, and they furnish a host of new criteria which must be applied in any attempt to explain and to appraise the Old Testament.

Two questions pose themselves immediately for solution. Firstly, what, if anything, do these three literatures owe to one another? And secondly, how do they compare with one another in form, content and literary value? The first of these questions has aroused considerable interest of late. The realization that the Hebrews were under definite obligations to Babylonia, or, more strictly speaking, to Sumeria, for some elements in their early legendary history, more particularly the episodes of the Creation and the Flood,

---

[1] Sethe, K., *Dramatische Texte zu altaegyptischen Mysterienspielen*, Leipzig, 1928.

and the striking parallels between the Sun-Hymn of Akhenaten and some of the Psalms, or between the Proverbs
of Amenope and those of Solomon, have produced lively
and fruitful discussion.[1] I shall not attempt to make any
contribution to this subject. I wish to occupy myself rather
with the second question, the comparison of the three
ancient literatures from the point of view of content, form,
and literary value. In one respect my treatment of this
subject must of necessity be lacking in balance. For many
years Egyptian literature has been my main field of study,
while that of Mesopotamia is known to me only from
translations. Consequently this work has a definite Egyptian bias. This needs the less excuse since I have in the
course of preparing the lectures become more than ever
convinced that the contribution made by Egypt to the
literature of the ancient world was very much greater than
that made by Mesopotamia. My object will have been
achieved if I can persuade students of the Old Testament
that Egyptian literature is worthy of far more attention at
their hands than it has hitherto received.

Let me at once confess, however, that the fault lies partly
with the Egyptologists themselves. The Old Testament,
like the New, has been singularly fortunate in its trans-

[1] The present state of the discussion is well summed up in two recent
books: Hugo Gressman and others, *The Psalmists*, Oxford, 1926, and
W. O. E. Oesterley, *The Wisdom of Egypt and the Old Testament*, London,
1927. On pp. 1–2 of the latter work is a good bibliography of English
and German books and articles dealing with the subject.

To these add now Paul Humbert, *Recherches sur les sources égyptiennes de
la littérature sapientale d'Israël*, Neuchâtel, 1929.

A good article by the late A. C. Mace, *The Influence of Egypt on Hebrew
Literature* in *Annals of Archaeology and Anthropology*, ix (Liverpool, 1922),
pp. 3 ff., has been overlooked by many subsequent writers.

Dr. A. S. Yahuda, in his recent work *Die Sprache des Pentateuch in ihren
Beziehungen zum Aegyptischen*, Erstes Buch, Berlin and Leipzig, 1929,
claims for Egypt a much more direct and fundamental influence on
early Hebrew literature than has ever previously been suggested. I
cannot agree with his conclusions, and have given my reasons in a re-
view of his book in *Journal of Egyptian Archaeology*, xvi, pp. 157-60.

lators. Their rendering is not always accurate—how could it be?—but from a literary point of view it is of the first order. It was a stroke of good fortune that the work should have been undertaken at a moment when the standard of writing among scholars and divines happened to be astonishingly high. Here we have an immensely long work which maintains almost throughout a style which has hardly ever been surpassed either before or since by the most accomplished writers of English prose. If the paucity of my acquaintance with Hebrew prevents me from saying that the work has gained by translation, my experience of literature in general enables me to assert confidently that it has not lost.

How different is the case with the literature of Egypt! The study of Ancient Egyptian is still in its infancy. It is only seven years since we made our pilgrimage to Grenoble to celebrate the hundredth anniversary of Champollion's epoch-making discovery. It is even less since the publication of the first Grammar of Middle Egyptian which can claim any approach to completeness,[1] and the Grammar of Late Egyptian is still to be written.[2] The first full dictionary of the language is even now not completed,[3] and needs revision and additions almost as fast as it appears. The number of scholars capable of making translations accurate enough to have any value whatsoever has always been very small, and it would be too much to expect that all, or even a large proportion, of these should combine literary gifts

[1] Gardiner, A. H., *Egyptian Grammar*, Oxford, 1927. The main lines of Middle Kingdom Egyptian Grammar were laid down 35 years ago by Adolf Erman in his *Ägyptische Grammatik*, of which the 4th edition appeared in 1928. The first edition of 1894 was followed five years later by Kurt Sethe's monumental study *Das Aegyptische Verbum*, Leipzig, 1899.

[2] It is a striking testimony to the paucity of workers in the field of Egyptian philology that Erman's *Neuaegyptische Grammatik*, published in 1880 and never reprinted, is the only existing work on the language of the New Kingdom.

[3] Erman, A. and Grapow, H., *Wörterbuch der aegyptischen Sprache*, Leipzig, in progress.

with philological. What is worse, these very men, anxious
to justify the accuracy of their renderings by showing precisely how they were obtained, have produced bald, stilted,
literal translations which may have their value for the
philologist, but which for the layman are often nearly unintelligible. Even the French, those masters in the handling
of words and sounds, fall under the same condemnation.
The result is that the outsider who wishes from the purely
literary point of view to get an insight into the literature of
Ancient Egypt turns back repelled, and very naturally
concludes that there is little to be said for it.

What is true of Egyptian is also true in a slightly smaller
degree of Babylonian, and, though in the translation of both
languages there are notable exceptions,[1] there can be no
doubt that the aridity of our renderings has largely deprived both of their due measure of consideration. The
fifty-third chapter of Isaiah, translated in the manner in
which most Egyptian papyri have been translated, would
be a commonplace piece of prose. The converse of this,
however, is not necessarily true, and it may be the case that
even the translators of our Bible would have failed to make
Egyptian literature a thing of beauty. At the same time it
remains true that in any discussion of the aesthetic value of
the Egyptian literature, above all in any attempt to compare it with that of the Hebrews, the inestimable superiority
of the biblical translation must be taken into account.

What is still more serious is that even those who know
Egyptian well are in very little better position to judge of its
aesthetic value than those who can read it only in translations. We may learn a foreign language well enough to
get considerable pleasure out of its literature, and to have
some appreciation of its beauty, but it would be absurd to
pretend that this appreciation can ever rival that which we
have of our own literature, where every word is surrounded

[1] An interesting literary experiment is R. Campbell Thompson's
Epic of Gilgamesh, London, 1928, a rendering of the Babylonian myth
into English hexameters.

by a mass of associations, conscious or half-conscious, where the most delicate shades of meaning are patent to us, and where not even the slightest allusion escapes us. A single instance will show what I mean. Professor A. C. Bradley amused the audience at his Inaugural Lecture in Oxford [1] by calling their attention to the havoc which would be wrought in Byron's lines

'Bring forth the horse!' The horse was brought:
In truth he was a noble steed!

by the transposition of the two words horse and steed, which ostensibly denote the same thing, but which in reality have entirely different associational and emotional contents. This is a gross example, but the finest distinctions of this kind, which are obvious enough to us in English, are far less obvious in French or German even to those of us who have long studied those languages, and in Egyptian I believe they are for the most part undiscernible even to the wisest. We have never heard or spoken Egyptian; we have not enough material, and what we have is too variable in date to allow any scholar to develop that fine literary sense which alone makes complete appreciation possible. Consequently even the scholar can get little more than the 'meaning' in the narrowest sense of the word; he misses most of the finer points, and is thus not so very much better off than the layman who must judge from his translation. As long as our ignorance is so great, our attitude towards the criticism of these ancient literatures must be one of extreme humility.

The literature of a people is the reflection of its mentality, and a people's mentality may be regarded as partly natural, or at least the product of causes far too remote in time to be observed by us, and partly the product of its known history. Consequently the literatures of the three peoples whom we are considering may be expected to show differences corresponding to the vicissitudes of their history. The Jews were in the main a nation of shepherds. The period during

[1] *Poetry for Poetry's Sake* (Oxford, 1901), p. 24.

which they produced their literature was one of continual stress and strain. Not only was their footing in Palestine insecure by reason of their turbulent immediate neighbours, but they dwelt in a land which had the misfortune to be a buffer between Egypt and Babylonia. That a small power should remain in this country independent of both of these mighty neighbours for any length of time was impossible, and it needed shrewd statesmanship to determine to which side it was safer to lean, and even then adhesion to the one power nearly always precipitated attack by the other. Was ever the political history of a people more tragic than this? And yet amid it all they preserved their confidence in themselves and in the great destiny which their God had in keeping for them. This deep religious faith, and the development of their worship into a lofty monotheism, set a stamp on their literature to which there is no parallel in Egypt or in Babylonia, where during the many centuries which produced literature little religious development is discernible.

Far different was the lot of the Egyptians. Settled in the land as agriculturalists from a remote date they felt themselves an old and established people. Though their own internal dissensions allowed the Delta to be invaded on two occasions, these incidents hardly touched the stability of Egypt's political power. The Nile Valley was hers and she knew it, and in it she built monuments which seemed almost as indestructible as the everlasting hills which lay on both sides of her. Her people were highly endowed both in science and art. Before 2000 B. C. they had found the area of the circle with an admirable approximation to accuracy, and produced portrait-statues in wood and stone, some of which remain among the world's masterpieces. They were a bright merry people with very little taint of cruelty in their nature, who loved wine and music and feasting. Their religious outlook, however, was deplorable. While they were keen ritualists, and most anxious as to their own welfare in the next world, it may be doubted whether at any

time any serious proportion of the people believed in good-
ness on earth as a passport to happiness in the life to come.
They were, finally, the most conservative nation in the
world; they never discarded anything as useless, even in the
domain of thought, and they would hold at one and the
same time two contradictory beliefs, or worship two deities
with directly opposed attributes, rather than consign anything to the scrap-heap.

The Babylonian Semites established themselves early in
Mesopotamia, but owed practically everything in the way
of art and culture to their predecessors the Sumerians.
Their literature has come down to us in copies of such varying dates that it is nearly impossible to trace any development in it,[1] and it is therefore difficult to say how much or
how little the Semites added to what the Sumerians be-
queathed to them. Certainly their attachment to the
Sumerian language seems to show that in the field of literature they felt little confidence in themselves. The situation is
complicated even further by the fact that much of the literature which has come down to us comes from Assyrian
sources, thus introducing into the problem a third, though
perhaps not wholly distinct, racial element. These difficulties combine to render somewhat obscure the connexion
between the literature of Babylonia and the peoples who
produced it.

The manner in which the varying mentality and history

---

[1] Weber writes (*Lit.*, p. 2): 'We are thus, in fact, faced with the
phenomenon that in Babylonian literature there is, broadly speaking,
neither archaic nor modern, nor any transition stages leading from the
one to the other ; the period of nearly 3,000 years through which the
monuments carry us shows in all essentials an unvarying picture of
intellectual life.' So, too, Meissner (*Lit.*, p. 2) says: 'Owing to these two
causes, its anonymous nature and its relatively small variation, it is
impossible to write a history of Babylonian-Assyrian literature connected with names of authors and displaying its development period by
period. We must for the time being be content to occupy ourselves with
the various categories of its literary output group by group, and to
examine them from the point of view of form and content.'

of these three great peoples whom I have so briefly characterized affected their literary product will, I hope, partly
appear in the course of these lectures. For the moment
there are one or two differences between the literatures as
they have come down to us which call for notice, but which
are the outcome rather of accident than of the character of
the peoples.

In the first place the literature of the Hebrews has come
to us by tradition, in the literal sense of the word; that of the
Egyptians and of the Babylonians by excavation. In the
two latter cases there has been no rigid artificial principle of
selection at work in determining what should survive and
what should not. The chance of excavation has been the
only force in play. Consequently we have a right to believe
that what has survived is in both cases a fair unselected
sample of what existed. There are doubtless surprises in
store for us in both countries, and we must never argue from
the absence of a particular form of literature that such form
was unknown. With this reservation, however, we are
justified in believing that the body of literature which has
come down to us from Egypt and from Babylonia is typical
and representative.

The case stands very differently with the Old Testament.
Here we have acquired nothing by excavation, but there
has been handed down to us a selection made with a very
definite and limited object, that of illustrating the religious
history of a single people. Consequently everything which
did not or was thought not to contribute to that end has
been rejected, and if a little has survived which does not
really fall under that category, like the Song of Solomon,
we have only the stupidity of the selectors to thank for our
good fortune. Thus the Old Testament literature is very
closely restricted in scope, and it possesses a unity which is
totally absent from the other two literatures which we are
studying; it is a particularly close-knit unity, for not only
are the books selected for their connexion with the national
religion, but they are to a great extent chosen because they

illustrate the development of that religion and the change in the people's attitude to its God. The Old Testament may thus be regarded as a dynamic rather than a static unity.

If Hebrew literature has in some ways gained by this selection it may in other ways have lost, for, though it is likely that in a highly religious community literature was very much the slave of religion, yet there are in what has survived hints of the existence of a profane literature of no little importance and value. Did such magnificent story-tellers know no stories but those of Abraham, Isaac, and Jacob, and were there no psalms in praise of wine and beauty? Did Botticelli paint no Venus and Michelangelo carve no Bacchus? In order to realize what we may have lost it is sufficient to turn to Egypt. Take away from Egyptian literature all that pertains even indirectly to religion and the worship of the gods, and there still remains enough to establish Egypt's claim to consideration as a literary nation. In other words, what has survived of Egyptian literature covers the whole field of thought and experience, what has survived of Hebrew covers a single field of thought, and, however predominant this field may have been in Hebrew life, the difference is fundamental and cannot be ignored.

On the other hand, the example of Babylonia warns us not to assume too readily the existence in Palestine of a large body of secular literature corresponding to that which forms the glory of the Egyptians. The tablets discovered in Babylonia, if we except those devoted to historical records and scientific treatises, are confined almost entirely to works directly or indirectly connected with religious ritual, that is to say, to epics dealing with the fortunes of gods and heroes, and lyrics in the form of prayers, psalms, hymns, and in-cantations. All these works are anonymous, and most of the versions we have are copies of originals of very great age. We have actually copies of the same work made at dates as much as 2,000 years apart. Since tablets of baked clay are not easily destructible we are led to ask whether the comparative lack of secular works is not to be explained rather by the supposition that such were rare than by the luck of survival. Does it not look as if literature in Babylonia was the bond-slave of that religion which permeated, far more than in Egypt, every department of life and thought? Further excavation may throw more light on this problem. In the meantime the absence of secular works in Babylonia, where no arbitrary principle of selection has been in play, should keep our minds open to the possibility that it is not entirely the taste of the makers of the Canon which has deprived us of works of this type from Palestine.

To the unity of purpose to which I have referred as marking the books of the Old Testament is to be added a comparative unity of time, if such a phrase may be allowed. The composition of the work all falls within a thousand years, and those the last millennium B.C. When we consider that modern literature covers no more than about 600 years this seems a long period, long enough to allow of more than one complete revolution in the thought of a nation. The literatures of Egypt and Babylon, however, cover a period of more than 3,000 years, of which 2,000 fall before the beginnings of the Old Testament.

Besides being a unity in the sense just described, the Old Testament has another advantage over its rivals. It has never died. It has been handed down through the ages, and there has never been a period when it was not being studied, when it was not influencing men's lives and ideas.[1] The race by and for whom it was written still exists in un-diminished strength, still plays an important part in the world's history. Babylonian on the other hand has been a dead language for over two millennia, and the race of Assurbanipal and Nebuchadnezzar is no more. The Egyptian hieroglyphs, too, died early in the Christian era, to be brought to life in the nineteenth century by the genius

[1] See G. A. Smith and others, *The Legacy of Israel* (Oxford, 1927), *passim*.

of Champollion. The language which they served to write did, it is true, survive for centuries in the form of Coptic, and Addison was not guilty of so wild an anachronism as might be thought when he regretted that he could not speak with his acquaintance the Egyptian merchant in the "modern Coptick."[1] Yet Coptic was the vehicle of a new religion and a new mode of thought, and can hardly be said to have carried on the tradition of Egyptian. So too, although the physical type of the ancient Egyptians survived the Mohammedan invasion, little of the glory of the Pharaohs survived with it.

How different has been the fate of the literature of the Jews! It has come down to us as part of our own literature, perhaps as the best-known part. From early childhood we have heard the deeds and misdeeds of the patriarchs read aloud in the church and in the home. The Old Testament is a field which is familiar to us, and one with which we have endless associations. Many of us know every corner of it. What is more, it has inspired much of the art and literature of modern and medieval Europe. Dante and Milton, Handel and Honegger have taken their subjects direct from it; there is practically no modern art which is not full of allusions to and illustrations from it,[2] and the whole of our culture is permeated with it.

Then again, it has not only been read to us, it has been commented on. Its obscurities and its difficulties have been explained to us, the background necessary to its comprehension has been reconstructed for us, and we can understand it and take it up into ourselves.

How stands the case with Egyptian or Babylonian? Put an Egyptian story before a layman, even in a good translation. He is at once in a strange land. The similes are pointless and even grotesque for him, the characters are strangers,

---

[1] *Spectator*, No. 69, May 19th, 1711. As a matter of fact, Addison probably used 'Coptick' not in its true linguistic sense, but merely with the meaning of Egyptian, i. e. Egyptian Arabic.

[2] G. A. Smith, *op. cit.*, pp. 433–505.

the background, the allusions, instead of delighting, only mystify and annoy. He lays it aside in disgust.

And lastly, the Old Testament possesses a personal interest which is almost wholly absent from the literatures of Egypt and Mesopotamia; we know the names of the authors of many of its books, and we know something of their history. Writers on Babylonian literature bewail the fact that it is wholly anonymous. Weber writes,[1] 'In the literary history of the whole world there is probably no other case in which a people, while exhibiting the highest literary activity conceivable, has failed to hand down with certainty the name of a single author.' Yet the case is little different in Egypt; the only works whose authors are named are the collections of aphorisms known as 'Instructions', and we are no more bound to believe that these, at any rate in their present form, were written by the men of old whose names they bear than we are bound to believe that the Book of Proverbs, as it stands, was the work of Solomon.

These are some of the essential external differences between the three literatures. Before we proceed to more intimate analysis one more point is still to be considered. The written or spoken word has two sides to it. It has sound, and it has meaning. In discussing aesthetic values the first of these must not be forgotten. When we speak of sound as an element in literature we mean that certain combinations of articulate sounds may be beautiful in themselves, quite apart from the thought which they convey. If, for instance, I say

A fancy from a flower-bell, some one's death,
A chorus-ending from Euripides,

the words mean very little as they stand, for the sentence of which they form a part is incomplete. Yet they have a beauty of their own; they are smooth, and they are easy to read. No doubt this quality could be partly analysed, and it would be found to depend upon the use of combinations of vowels and consonants which are naturally easy to pro-

[1] *Lit.*, p. 2.

nounce and pleasant to hear, and the avoidance of such as
are not.[1] The poet may not analyse, but he is well aware of
the importance of these harmonies. Swinburne was perhaps
our greatest master in this art, though he sometimes allowed
sound to obscure sense.

Now this quality is, by those best qualified to judge, held
to exist in a high degree in Hebrew poetry. Dr. George
Adam Smith called attention to it in his Schweich Lectures
in 1910,[2] and he also remarked on the admirable adaptation
of rhythm and sound to the subject in hand. I do not know
that any similar observations have been made in regard to
Babylonian. In the case of Egyptian we are most unfortunately prevented from applying any test of this kind. In the
first place the exact pronunciation of some of the consonants
cannot be fixed. Secondly the writing of Egyptian is so
variable that it is often impossible to reconstruct even the
consonantal skeleton of a word with certainty. What is
worst of all is that the vowels were not written, and that, in
spite of some very ingenious research based on cuneiform
equivalents of Egyptian words, and on the vowels in Coptic,
which are fully written, we still know almost nothing of the
quality of the vowels in Egyptian, though we do know
certain rules which governed their quantity.[3]

These difficulties, and in particular our ignorance of the
vowel sounds, make it practically impossible to form any
idea whatsoever of the sound or even the rhythm of
Egyptian prose and poetry. Judging by the analogy of
other literatures, this property of rhythm is one which
rarely fails to develop quite early. Consequently we have
good reason to believe that Egyptian possessed it, and it

[1] No one knew this better than Browning himself when, with delightful malice, he wrote:

> *Irks care the crop-full bird,*
> *Frets doubt the maw-crammed beast?*

[2] *The Early Poetry of Israel in its Physical and Social Origins* (London,
1912), pp. 5–7.

[3] See Sethe, *Die Vokalisation des Ägyptischen* (*Zeitschr. d. Deutsch.
Morgenl. Gesellschaft*), Band 77 (1923).

may be surmised that, if we could read some of the finest of the Egyptian papyri as they were read by their writers, instead of transferring them to paper as a bald skeleton of consonants interspersed with queries, we should think even more highly of Egyptian than we do. As it is, no comparison in this respect with either Hebrew or Babylonian is possible.

We are now free to begin our survey of Egyptian literature. Pieper remarks at the outset of his recent admirable sketch[1] that he has often been asked by an astonished layman, But is there an Egyptian literature, in a sense that there is a Greek or a Latin or a German literature? And we have all had this same experience. Yes, there is an Egyptian literature, and a very extensive and varied one. And it is a literature in the sense that the Greek and the Latin are, that is to say, it comprises not merely historical inscriptions, records of facts, and scientific treatises, but also works which have literary value quite apart from practical purpose, works which show us that the Egyptian had a full appreciation of literature for its own sake and that he knew what was meant by style.[2]

[1] Max Pieper, *Die aegyptische Literatur* (Wildpark-Potsdam, 1927), in the series *Handbuch der Literaturwissenschaft*, edited by Oskar Walzel. It is astonishing that this should be the first attempt ever made to assess the literary value of the Egyptian papyri as a whole. Adolf Erman's *Die Literatur der Aegypter* (Leipzig, 1923) is a volume of translations covering practically the whole of the field, and it has been translated into English by A. M. Blackman under the title, Adolf Erman, *The Literature of the Ancient Egyptians* (London, 1927). The best of the religious literature will be found translated in G. Roeder, *Urkunden zur Religion des alten Ägypten* (Jena, 1915).

I should like here to pay my tribute to Hermann Grapow's clever and valuable *Die bildlichen Ausdrücke des Aegyptischen, Vom Denken und Dichten einer altorientalischen Sprache* (Leipzig, 1924) which breaks entirely new ground in the treatment of Egyptian.

[2] How totally Egyptian literature is still misunderstood, even in learned quarters, is shown by the following strange quotation from a publisher's advertisement of a book—and a good book—on a section

Of the mass of written material which has come down to us we may for the purposes of the present inquiry dismiss certain sections very shortly. In the first place we may set aside the whole category of historical inscriptions, records set up by kings on stelae or on temple walls, biographies of nobles and soldiers written on their tombstones. I do not mean to say that these never have literary qualities. They have; but they are, as it were, the stronghold of formality and stiltedness in expression, and, vast though the quantity of material is, it forms but an insignificant part of Egypt's contribution to literature.

Next come the scientific papyri. Here we have two long mathematical papyri and at least five medical. These, too, lie outside our scope, and I mention them only for the sake of completeness. The mathematical works are mainly collections of problems worked out to serve as models for the solution of other problems with similar data; the medical are at their best dry catalogues of symptoms, diagnoses and remedies, and at their worst mere collections of magical spells for the banishment of disease or death. They again have no literary value.

Papyri containing accounts, very numerous, and valuable for the study of social conditions, need only a passing mention.

Records of famous trials, such as that of the criminals in the harem conspiracy against Ramesses III, and that of the royal-tomb-robbers at the end of the XXth Dynasty, again have their value, but it is not literary. The same may be said of the longest and most beautiful papyrus in the world, that known as the Great Harris Papyrus, now in the

of Babylonian literature, by one who is an authority on his subject. 'Die ägyptische Seele offenbart ihre Symbolik vornehmlich in der Kunst, die sumerisch-babylonische in der Literatur. Auf dem Gebiete der Kunst stehen die Ägypter höher als die Babylonier. Wenn man aber die vorliegende Schrift . . . liest und damit die Literatur der Ägypter vergleicht, wird man sehen, dass auf dem literarischen Gebiete die euphratensische Kultur ihre Schwester am Nil weit überholt hat.'

British Museum, which records the benefactions of King Ramesses III to the temples of Egypt.

Letters, too, may be set aside, with the exception of such model letters as it was customary to produce in the writing-schools by way of literary exercises. To these we shall return later.

It may also be of interest to remark here that we have no records of laws, nothing, that is, to compare with Deuteronomy, except a stela with some special enactments of Horemheb, first king of the XIXth Dynasty, designed to cope with the chaotic situation which he found in Egypt on his accession to the throne. Apart from this we know nothing of the laws of Ancient Egypt, neither who made them, nor how they were recorded. There is, however, in the tomb of the vizier Rekhmire, who lived in the XVIIIth Dynasty, a long inscription embodying instructions to the vizier for the conduct of the business of the land, not altogether devoid of literary interest, from which we learn that the law was laid before him in his court of justice written on forty rolls, probably of leather.

The rest of the material, that which constitutes Egyptian literature in the narrower sense of the term, may be divided into four classes: epic, lyric, dramatic, and didactic, and in this order we shall deal with it.

In the domain of epic both the Mesopotamian and the Hebrew civilizations made an immense contribution to literature. In both countries the exploits of the great national heroes, mythical, semi-mythical, and wholly real, were worked up into serial form. From Babylonia we have already a large number of such works in metrical form, the epic of Enuma Elish, the myth of Etana, the epic of Gilgamesh, and Ishtar's journey to the Underworld. The roots of this literature go back into Sumerian times, and it is beyond doubt the earliest body of epic poetry which has survived.

In Palestine too we find a cycle of epic of a much less self-conscious type. There is general agreement that in some of

its earlier episodes, more especially those of the Flood and
the Creation, it is not independent of that of Babylonia, but
in so far as it recounts the deeds of the great ancestors of the
Hebrews its content is original. In date, however, it is
manifestly much later, none of it having been committed
to writing, at least in its present form, until more than
two thousand years after the earliest of the Babylonian
epic.

This epic forms one of the Hebrews' greatest contributions
to literature. Its extent, its variety, the perfection of its
simplicity, its descriptive power, all help to make it un-
surpassed and perhaps unsurpassable.

When we turn to Egypt in the expectation of finding
there something with which to compare this phenomenon
in Palestine and Babylonia we meet with disappointment.
Egypt has no great body of national epic, or, to be exact,
none such has been preserved for us. That it existed may be
regarded as beyond doubt, for not only does the analogy of
all early civilized peoples lead us to assume it, but there are
in Egyptian definite hints of its existence. Thus there was
certainly a vast body of myth collected round the Sun-god;
fragments of it have survived. Such, for example, are the
story of the destruction of mankind,[1] and the stratagem by
which Isis prevailed upon Re to disclose his secret name.[2]

---

[1] The text known as The Destruction of Mankind forms part of a book
of magic spells, inscribed in the tombs of Seti I and Ramesses III. See
Transactions of the Society of Biblical Archaeology, iv, pp. 1 ff. and viii, pp.
412 ff. Translated by Roeder, *Urkunden*, etc., pp. 142 ff.

[2] The hieratic papyrus which contains this legend has been published in facsimile in F. Rossi and W. Pleyte, *Papyrus de Turin* (Leyden,
1869–1876), Plates 31, 77, and 131–8. Other fragments of solar
mythology have been collected from late temple inscriptions by H.
Junker in his *Auszug der Hathor-Tefnut aus Nubien* (*Anhang zu den Abhandlungen der Berliner Akademie*, 1911). See, too, Sethe in *Untersuchungen zur
Geschichte und Altertumskunde Aegyptens*, V. Band, Heft 3, *Zur altägyptischen
Sage vom Sonnenauge das in der Fremde war*, and Spiegelberg's publication
of the Leyden demotic papyrus I. 384, which deals with the same
myth, *Der ägyptische Mythus vom Sonnenauge* (Strassburg, 1917).

What a mass of legend too must in all periods have clustered round the figures of Horus and Set! A late papyrus, still unpublished,[1] reveals episodes in this myth hitherto undreamed of, and Plutarch, when he came to write his *Isis and Osiris*, found no dearth of material. Chance has certainly been unkind to us in the matter of Egyptian myth, and comparatively little has survived. Much there must have been, but we are not in a position to say whether it had any of the high qualities which characterize the epics of Babylonia and Palestine.

As an example of Egyptian epic we may take the story of how Isis betrayed Re into telling her his secret name. It is preserved, as part of a magic spell against snake-bite, in a papyrus of New Empire date, now in Turin. It should be explained that in Egyptian, as in most other magic, the knowledge of a person's name gave to him who possessed it magical power over the person himself; hence the anxiety of Re to conceal his name, and of Isis to make him reveal it.

Now Isis was a woman wise of speech. Her heart was more cunning than millions of men, she was wiser (?) than millions of gods and she was the equal (?) of millions of spirits. She knew all that was in heaven and in earth, like Re who accomplishes the needs of earth. And the goddess planned in her heart to learn the name of the august god.

Now Re entered heaven each day at the head of the crew[2], and sate him down upon the Throne of the Two Horizons. But divine old age caused his mouth to overflow (?) so that he spat upon the earth, and his spittle fell upon the ground. And Isis scraped it together (?) in her hand, with the earth which was upon it. She made it into a lordly snake and moulded it in the form of a . . . . Yet it moved not as alive

---

[1] Chester Beatty Papyrus No. 1, shortly to be published by Dr. A. H. Gardiner.

[2] I. e. the crew of the boat in which the Sun-god was believed to cross the heaven daily.

before her but lay on the road on which the great god was wont to walk according to his desire through his Two Lands.

Now the august god came forth in splendour, and the gods in the Palace in his train, to walk abroad as he did every day. And the lordly snake bit him, even the living fire that came forth from himself. . . . And the divine god uttered his voice, and the sound of his majesty reached the heaven, so that his Ennead[1] cried, What is it? What is it? and his gods, What? What? Yet could he not find voice to answer. His lips trembled and all his limbs quaked, for the poison had taken hold upon his flesh even as the Nile takes hold upon . . .[2]

Now when the great god had controlled his heart again he cried to his following, Come to me, ye who came into being out of my body, ye gods that came out of me, that I may tell you what has happened. An evil thing hath stung me. My heart knoweth it ⟨not⟩, mine eyes see it not, my hand made it not, and I know it not among all that I created. I have felt no pain like unto it, and there is naught more painful. I am a prince, the son of a prince; the seed of a god which had its being from a god. I am a great one, son of a great one. My father devised my name. I am one who has many names and many forms. My form is in every god. Tum and Horus-Hekenu are invoked ⟨in me⟩. My father and my mother gave me my name, and it has lain hidden in my body since I was born, that no sorcerer or sorceress should have power over me. Now as I came forth to behold what I have created and to walk abroad in the Two Lands which I formed something that I know not stung me. It is not fire, it is not water; yet my heart burns, my body trembles and all my limbs are chilled (?). Send to me the divine children who possess speech which availeth, wise of tongue, whose cunning reaches to heaven.

Then the divine children came to him, each of them with his lament (?). And Isis, too, came with her service, whose counsel is the breath of life, whose sayings drive out sickness, and whose word gives life to him whose breath is failing. She said, What is it? What is it? Divine father, What? If a snake hath done thee an injury (?) or

---

[1] The cycle of nine gods of which Re was the chief.

[2] The words which stand here, *in his train*, make no sense. Has something been omitted?

*a creature of thine raised its head against thee, I will cast him down
by potent magic and prevent him from beholding thy rays.*

*Then the august god opened his mouth ⟨and said⟩, I was going
upon the road, walking in the Two Lands and on the desert, for my
soul was fain to behold that which I created, and lo, I was stung by
a snake which I saw not. It is not fire, it is not water; yet am
I colder than water and hotter than fire. My whole body sweats, and
I tremble. My eye is not firm, and I cannot see, for water rains down
my face as in the heat of summer.*

*Then Isis said to Re. Tell me thy name, divine father, for the
man in whose name a spell is recited shall live. And Re made answer,
I am he that made heaven and earth, that put together the hills and
created that which is thereon. I am he that made the water, and
Mehwert came into being; that made the bull for the cow, and the
Begetter came into being. I am he that formed the heaven and the
secrets of the Two Horizons, and set the Spirits of the Gods therein.
I am he that opened his eyes, and light came into being; that closed his
eyes, and darkness came into being; at whose command the Nile flows.
The gods know not his name. I am he who made the hours, and the
days came into being; I am he who opened the yearly festivals and
created the stream. I am he who made the fire of life to create the
works of the . . . . I am Khepri in the morning, Re at his noon, and
Atum in the evening.*

*Yet the poison was not driven from its course, nor the plight of the
great god assuaged. Then said Isis to Re, Thy name is not among all
that thou hast said to me. Tell it to me that the poison may go forth.
The man whose name is pronounced shall live. Now the poison
burned fiercely, it became mightier than flame or fire. And the
majesty of Re said, Lend me ⟨thine⟩ ears, O daughter Isis, and my
name shall pass from my body into thy body. Then the god hid himself[1] from the gods, for wide was the space in the Bark of Millions
of Years.[2] And when the moment of revealing the heart was come she
said to ⟨her⟩ son Horus, Make him powerless for me by an oath that
the god give up his two eyes. So the great god revealed his name to
Isis. ⟨And Isis⟩ the great magician ⟨said⟩, Poisonous flux (?), Come*

---

[1] Or 'it', i. e. the name.

[2] The sun-bark in which Re and his suite daily cross the sky.

forth from Re. O Eye of Horus, come forth from the god, . . . spittle
of the mouth. I am one who accomplishes; I am one who sends.
Come on to the ground. Mighty poison, see, the great god hath re-
vealed his name. Re lives, and the poison is dead. So-and-so son of
So-and-so[1] lives, and the poison is dead. So spake Isis the great,
the princess of the gods, who knew Re by his real name.

This is not good story-telling. The movement is slow,
there is too much extraneous mythological detail, and the
main points of the action are obscured by the wordiness of
the speeches. How bad it is will be clearly seen if it be
compared with an incident in the Old Testament which
bears a superficial resemblance to it in content, namely the
raising up by Moses of the brazen serpent (Numbers xxi.
4–9). Here a story which contains little less than the
Egyptian is told in six verses; we are given everything that
is essential, and there is not a superfluous word.

We have, however, another Egyptian story of the old age
of the sun-god which, although far from perfect, realizes
some of the qualities of epic which are lacking in that of Isis
and Re. Like this latter it owes its survival to the fact that
it was taken up into a book of spells; as part of this book, it
was inscribed in the tombs of Seti I of the XIXth Dynasty
and Ramesses III of the XXth. Both texts are damaged,
but from a combination of the two the story can be restored
almost complete. It tells how, when Re the sun-god grew
old, mankind plotted to overthrow him. Thereupon he sent
the goddess Hathor, who is identified in myth with his eye,
to destroy mankind. After the work of destruction had
begun, however, he repented, and devised a scheme to save
the remainder from the fury of the goddess.[2]

---

[1] In a magic spell as prescribed in the books of magic the name of
the patient is naturally given as So-and-so son of So-and-so, and is to
be filled in by the user of the spell. But it is clearly quite out of place
in the present passage.

[2] I have used Naville's texts, *Transactions of the Soc. of Bibl. Archaeology*,
iv, pp. 1–19 and five unnumbered plates; viii, pp. 412–20, Pls. 1–3.
Fresh copies of the originals are badly needed.

... *the god who created himself, when he was king over both gods and men. Mankind devised a plot. Now his majesty had waxed old, his bones were silver, his flesh gold, and his hair real lapis lazuli.*[1]

Now his majesty perceived that which was being devised against him by mankind. And his majesty said to them that were in his suite, Come, call to me mine Eye, and Shu, and Tefnut, and Geb, and Nut, together with the fathers and mothers that were with me when I was yet in Nun,[2] *and likewise my god Nun himself. Let him bring his courtiers with him. Thou shalt bring them in secret, lest mankind should see and their hearts take fright. Thou shalt come with them to the Great Castle that they may give their advice.*[3]

So these gods were brought. And these gods came before him, touching the earth with their foreheads in the presence of his majesty, that he might speak his words in the presence of the Father of the Eldest Ones,[4] *even him that fashioned mankind, the king of men.*

They said to his majesty, Speak to us that we may hear it. And Re said unto Nun, O eldest god, in whom I came into being, and ye gods of old, Behold, mankind, who came into being in my eye,[5] *they have devised a plot against me; tell me what I may do concerning it. Lo, I am yet seeking, and I will not slay them until I hear what ye have to say concerning it. Then the majesty of Nun said, My son Re, thou god greater than he that created him, older than they that fashioned him, abide where thou art; great is the fear of thee if but thine eye be turned against them that imagine evil against thee. And the majesty of Re said, But behold they are fled into the desert, their hearts being afraid for what they have said. And they said to his majesty, Send forth thine Eye that it may slay them for thee ... to slay them for thee when she descends as Hathor.*

So this goddess returned, when she had slain mankind in the desert. Said the majesty of this god, Welcome, welcome, Hathor, thou hast done that for which I sent thee. And this goddess said, As

---

[1] Apparently symptoms of age in a god.

[2] The primeval ocean from which he emerged.

[3] An obscure and perhaps misplaced sentence follows.

[4] I. e., Nun.

[5] Re wept and his tears became men. This legend is based on a pun between *rmt* 'men' and *rmyt* 'tears'.

*thou livest I have prevailed over mankind and my heart rejoices
thereat. . . .* [1]

*And Re said, Come, call unto me swift-speeding messengers, that
they may run like the shadow of a body. And these messengers were
brought forthwith. And the majesty of this god said, Haste ye to
Elephantine and bring me much red ochre. And this red ochre was
brought to him. And the majesty of this great god gave command to
Him-with-the-sidelock, who is in Heliopolis, to grind this red ochre.
Then the maidservants bruised barley for beer, and this red ochre was
added to this mash, and it was like human blood. And seven thousand hebent-jugs of beer were made ready.*

*Now the majesty of the King of Upper and Lower Egypt Re came
along with these gods to see this beer. And the day dawned on which
the goddess was to slay mankind, at the season of their going up
stream. Said the majesty of this god, It is exceeding good, I will
protect mankind therewith(?). And Re said, Bear it now to the
place wherein she said that she would slay mankind. And the
majesty of the King of Upper and Lower Egypt Re rose up early in
the depth of night to have this sleeping-draught(?) poured out; and
the fields which . . . were filled with liquor through the might of the
majesty of this god.*

*And in the morning the goddess went and found them flooded.
And her face was beautiful therein. She drank, and it was pleasant
in her heart. She became drunk and knew not mankind.*

Whether these extracts are typical of what is best or of
what is worst, from the literary point of view, in the epic of
the Egyptian gods and heroes, we cannot say. They are
virtually our only examples, and by them Egypt's achievement in this branch of writing must be judged.

When we compare these with the earliest episodes in the
saga of the Hebrews we are struck at once with a difference
which is not strictly literary, but which nevertheless cannot
be ignored in comparing the literary value of the two epics.
In both, divine beings take an active part, but, while in the

---

[1] Here follows an obscure passage which, to judge by what follows,
should record Re's repentance of his design and his resolve to save some
remnant of mankind; it does not, however, seem to do so.

Egyptian stories they are creatures with the same passions as men, who grow old and infirm, who love and hate, and have their private feuds, in the Hebrew stories, crude though they be, there is but one god, who is never represented as acting in a manner unworthy of a very high conception of godhead. He may seem unduly severe in punishing disobedience, but he is never mean or petty. This gives to the story of Noah a lofty dignity which The Destruction of Mankind completely lacks, and this dignity becomes in itself a literary merit.

Quite apart from this, however, no one who reads these two stories can fail to see the infinite superiority of the Noah legend as a piece of narration and description. It is free from all those tiresome mythological allusions with which the multiplicity of the Egyptian pantheon overloads and obscures the most straightforward legend; it is more natural and probable, and above all it is a more vivid and convincing description.[1] It makes us fellow witnesses of the scene and calls up a clear picture of its most lively details. If the Destruction of Mankind represents Egyptian epic at its best, then the palm must go to the Hebrews.

But here we must be very cautious. The Hebrew account of the Deluge is admittedly based directly on the Mesopotamian flood-story, known to us from the episode of Utnapishtim in the Gilgamesh epic and from fragments of a much earlier Sumerian version.[2] What is more, the very features which attracted us in the biblical story are present in the Mesopotamian. It would seem therefore as if the palm which the Hebrews have won from the Egyptians belongs of right to the Babylonians or the Sumerians. Yet this is not necessarily the case. The episodes which the Hebrews owed to Babylonia are, so far as we know, two only, the Creation and the Flood, and, even if future

---

[1] It must not be forgotten that the story of Noah as we have it in Genesis combines two versions. See Driver, *Book of Genesis*, pp. 85 ff.

[2] See L. W. King's Schweich Lectures for 1916, *Legends of Babylon and Egypt in relation to Hebrew Tradition*, pp. 41 ff.

E

excavation should add to these, it is manifest that the greater part of the story of the patriarchs is purely national, and can owe nothing to outside influence. Yet the high standard of writing which we have praised in the Flood story is kept up throughout the rest of the Pentateuch, as well as in the more definitely historical portions of the Old Testament. We may thus safely assert that, even if the Hebrews in their attempts to set down their early history borrowed portions of Mesopotamian legend and copied directly the original wording, they rapidly evolved for themselves a narrative style of a high order.[1] It will, indeed, probably be agreed that in the mere matter of narration they out-distanced their models. Yet one thing must not be overlooked. The Hebrew was intent on telling in simple and direct language the history of his people, and the Old Testament is a series of historical stories, briefly and excellently told; it is not an epic in the true sense. The Babylonian set out with a different object. He was working up the story of the demigods and heroes for use in the service of religion. Here brevity was no object, and the discursiveness which is a feature of all true epic was in place. The mere fact that metrical form was used shows that this was conscious art. Thus Babylonia and not Palestine created epic, and the true forerunners of the *Iliad* and the *Divina Commedia* were not Genesis and Exodus but the legends of Etana and Gilgamesh.

The result of the foregoing discussion may be summed up as follows: Babylonia invented the epic as a literary form at a very early date; the Hebrews, at first perhaps under the influence of their Mesopotamian neighbours, developed admirable powers of story-telling, which they employed in writing down the national history; of the Egyptians it can only be said that the small body of myth and legend which

---

[1] It is a striking fact that this excellence is common to the three most important of the documents of which the Pentateuch is composed, namely J, E and P, though the last falls a little short of the standard of the other two.

they have left us rivals neither that of the Babylonians as epic, nor that of the Hebrews as story-telling.[1]

While, however, Egyptian epic has almost wholly perished, there is no dearth of short stories, and if we wish to compare the narrative powers of the Egyptians with those of the Hebrews and Babylonians we shall have on the Egyptian side to draw our illustrations from short stories, while on the other side we must have recourse to the great epics. From the modern point of view this is unfair. The origins of the modern novel and the modern short story seem to be quite distinct. While the former is the outcome of the picaresque epics, if I may so call them, of Cervantes and Grimmelshausen, followed closely by Le Sage's *Gil Blas* and Richardson's *Clarissa*, the latter seems to have arisen out of the short character-sketches of the periodical essayists. In early literature we should expect to find this distinction much less marked. And so it is in the Old Testament, which, as we have just seen, is a collection of short stories. We wrong neither the Egyptian nor the Hebrew when, for purposes of comparison, we regard the episode of Joseph as a complete story in itself. We must, however, be more cautious in the case of Babylonia, for her stories are integral parts of a literary form, the epic. It is not fair to them to pluck them from their context and to compare them with short stories as such.

Egypt, on the other hand, is the home of the short story, and one of her claims to literary recognition is that she produced the first short stories to be told for their own sake. Her stories are pure pastime, not propagandist or aetiological in origin. Ruth and Jonah were written as protests against the growing insularity of Judaism; Esther was invented to explain the origin of the feast of Purim. The Egyptian told his tales for the pure joy of story-telling.

[1] For an appreciation of the Hebrew power of story-telling see P. C. Sands, *Literary Genius of the Old Testament* (Oxford, 1924), a book well worth careful study.

One of the earliest Egyptian stories which have come down to us is that known as The Shipwrecked Sailor, dating from the Middle Kingdom. Its content is very simple: an Egyptian sailor goes down to a port on the Red Sea to take ship for some mining country, possibly Sinai, on an errand for his king. The ship meets a storm and is wrecked, and he alone is saved. He is cast on a desert island, where he is terrified by the appearance of a huge snake, the presiding genius of the island. The sailor's fears are, however, vain, for the snake treats him kindly, relates for his comfort an adventure of his own from which he escaped unscathed, and assures him that a ship will come from Egypt and take him safely home. And this prophecy indeed comes to pass.

Such is the story, but it has a setting. It is represented as being related by a sailor to his captain on board a ship sent up the Nile on an expedition, probably commercial, which has proved unsuccessful. The captain looks forward with dread to his meeting with the Pharaoh, when he must confess his failure, and the sailor seeks to comfort him with this story of misfortune ending happily. At the end of the piece, however, we find the captain refusing the proffered comfort with the remark, *Who giveth water at dawn to the bird that is to be slaughtered the same morning?*, which would seem to mean 'I am doomed to die when I meet Pharaoh, and so your comfort is wasted on me'.

Here we have passed the age of simple story-telling, as the existence of a setting in itself suffices to show. Yet the style is simple and straightforward: [1]

I will relate to thee something like it which happened to me myself, when I went to the mining country for the sovereign, and went down to the ocean in a ship 150 cubits long and 40 cubits broad, in which were 50 sailors of the chosen of Egypt. Whether they looked at the

[1] From a papyrus in the Hermitage in Leningrad, published by Golenishchef in *Recueil de travaux*, xxviii, pp. 73 ff.; later by Erman in *Zeitschrift für äg. Sprache*, xliii, pp. 1 ff. Good notes by Gardiner in the same *Zeitschrift*, xlv, 60 ff., and Dévaud, *Recueil de travaux*, xxxviii, pp. 188 ff.

heaven or whether they looked at the earth their hearts were stouter than lions.

They foretold a storm ere it came, a tempest before it had yet come to pass. The storm broke while we were still at sea, before we could reach the land. The wind rose and redoubled its fury. It brought a wave eight cubits in height. I was borne overboard with the mast.[1] The ship perished and they that were in it; not one of them was left.

I was cast upon an island by a wave of the sea. I spent three days alone with my heart for my companion. I slept in a shelter of wood: I embraced the shade. Then I stood upon my feet to find what I might put in my mouth. I found figs and grapes there and every kind of fine vegetables. There were kau *and* nekut *and gherkins as if cultivated;[2] there were fish there and birds. There is nothing which was not therein. I sated myself and left some lying on the ground, for it was too heavy for my arms. I took a fire-drill and made fire, and offered a burnt-offering to the gods.*

Then I heard a thunderous noise and thought it was a wave of the sea. Trees brake and the earth trembled. When I had uncovered my face I found it was a serpent who was drawing nigh. Thirty cubits long was he, and his beard was more than five cubits in length. His body was overlaid with gold, and his eyebrows were of true lapis lazuli. And he was exceeding wise.

The serpent now demands the reason for the stranger's presence on the island. The sailor repeats his story in the same words in which we have already heard it, and the tale continues:

Then said he unto me, Fear not, fear not, little one. Let not thy heart be troubled, now that thou art come to me. Behold, God hath kept thee alive that he might bring thee to this isle of plenty, where there is nothing which doth not grow, for it is full of every good thing. Lo, thou shalt pass month after month until thou shalt have accomplished four months on this island. A ship shall come from Egypt, with sailors therein whom thou knowest, and thou shalt return home with them. In thine own city shalt thou die.

[1] This sentence is unintelligible. My paraphrase is based on a suggestion of Dr. A. M. Blackman.

[2] Blackman's admirable suggestion.

As story-telling this has some good qualities. The action moves rapidly, and there is little that is unessential; the check caused by the sailor's repeating a considerable portion of the story to the snake, instead of simply saying 'Then I told him what had befallen me' or something of that kind, would be felt far less by the ancient mind, which was not troubled by much sense of time limit, than it is by the modern. Such repetition is commonplace in all early story-writing.[1] There is imagination and power of description. The storm, the desert island and the snake himself are all well treated, and drawn each in a few skilful traits,[2] though in enumerating the products of the island the writer cannot resist the temptation, yielded to by all early story-tellers, to reduce description to a mere catalogue.[3] There is considerable dramatic power, nowhere better shown than in the description of the arrival of the ship from Egypt:

And the ship came, even as he had foretold. And I went and got me up into a high tree, and I recognized them that were in it. Then I went to tell it to him and I found that he knew it.

This is admirable and in the best vein of story-telling.

[1] E. g. Genesis xxiv. 3–8 and 37–41.

[2] It is instructive to contrast this description with Vergil's account of the two serpents who attacked Laocoon and his sons (*Aen.* ii. 203 ff.).

> *Ecce autem gemini a Tenedo tranquilla per alta*
> *(horresco referens) immensis orbibus angues*
> *incumbunt pelago, pariterque ad litora tendunt;*
> *pectora quorum inter fluctus arrecta iubaeque*
> *sanguineae superant undas, pars cetera pontum*
> *pone legit sinuatque immensa volumine terga.*
> *Fit sonitus spumante salo; iamque arva tenebant,*
> *ardentesque oculos suffecti sanguine et igni*
> *sibila lambebant linguis vibrantibus ora.*

The Egyptian gives only the bare essentials, the noise, the fact of the snake's approach, his measurements, the material of which he was made and his intelligence. Vergil spares us no single detail of the scene and the effect which it produced on the minds of those who saw it.

[3] Cf. 'the sound of the cornet, flute, harp, sackbut, psaltery, and all kinds of musick'.

The Story of the Shipwrecked Sailor is in no sense a psychological novel. There is little attempt to draw the character of either sailor or snake, there is no moral development, and any psychological interest there may be lies in the purpose of the sailor's story, which is to comfort his leader by reciting the happy issue of an adventure of his own. There is nothing very deep or subtle about this, and when the snake proceeds in his turn to act as comforter to the sailor on precisely similar lines the artifice becomes a little threadbare.

One other trait deserves mention. The Egyptian loved, as we shall see later, to moralize. Egyptian conversation, if we may judge from the literature, must have been full of old saws produced in and out of season. *When you face the king*, says the sailor to his leader, *speak out boldly. It is a man's mouth that saveth him, and his speech that causeth men to respect him.* This is a wise enough remark in itself, but one feels that it had been made before and would be made again. Similarly the snake, having heard the sailor's story, and being about to relate his own, cannot refrain from moralizing: *How happy is he who tells what he hath suffered when the evil moment is past.* The sailor, too, in concluding his story to his leader is entitled to remark *Do thou hearken to what I say*, but has hardly the right to add *It is good for men to hearken*:[1] this is a little too trite.

One more criticism. The sailor promises to send the snake offerings consisting of various kinds of incense, including *antiu* and *hekenu*, whatever these may be. The snake smiles at his folly, and tells him that *hekenu* is the chief product of the island, and that, moreover, he himself happens to be lord of the *antiu*-bearing country of Punt. The sailor's promised gifts would thus be coals to New-castle. This incident is an excrescence. It has no relation to the rest of the story and it holds up the action. It is probably an allusion to some myth concerning a serpent-

[1] Cf. the Proverbs of Ptahhotep, *To hearken is better than anything that is.*

god and the land of Punt, and the mythologist has here got the better of the story-teller, to the disadvantage of the story.

Let us now turn for a moment from Egypt to Palestine. Take almost at random a portion of the great epic which describes the lives of the patriarchs. Here is the fiftieth chapter of Genesis, relating the mourning for and burial of Jacob.

1. And Joseph fell upon his father's face, and wept upon him, and kissed him.

2. And Joseph commanded his servants the physicians to embalm his father: and the physicians embalmed Israel.

3. And forty days were fulfilled for him; for so are fulfilled the days of those which are embalmed: and the Egyptians mourned for him threescore and ten days.

4. And when the days of his mourning were past, Joseph spake unto the house of Pharaoh, saying, If now I have found grace in your eyes, speak, I pray you, in the ears of Pharaoh, saying,

5. My father made me swear, saying, Lo, I die: in my grave which I have digged for me in the land of Canaan, there shalt thou bury me. Now therefore let me go up, I pray thee, and bury my father, and I will come again.

6. And Pharaoh said, Go up, and bury thy father, according as he made thee swear.

7. And Joseph went up to bury his father: and with him went up all the servants of Pharaoh, the elders of his house, and all the elders of the land of Egypt,

8. And all the house of Joseph, and his brethren, and his father's house: only their little ones, and their flocks, and their herds, they left in the land of Goshen.

9. And there went up with him both chariots and horsemen: and it was a very great company.

10. And they came to the threshingfloor of Atad, which is beyond Jordan, and there they mourned with a great and very sore lamentation: and he made a mourning for his father seven days.

11. And when the inhabitants of the land, the Canaanites, saw the mourning in the floor of Atad, they said, This is a grievous mourning to the Egyptians: wherefore the name of it was called Abel-mizraim, which is beyond Jordan.

12. And his sons did unto him according as he commanded them:

13. For his sons carried him into the land of Canaan, and buried him in the cave of the field of Machpelah, which Abraham bought with the field, for a possession of a buryingplace, of Ephron the Hittite, before Mamre.

Was story ever better told? All is crystal clear. Every sentence, every word almost, advances the action, and there is never a check except to explain what would otherwise be unintelligible, such as the 'forty days' which were fulfilled for Jacob. No doubt verse 11 is nothing more than an archaeological explanation of the place-name Abel-miz-raim, 'mourning of the Egyptians'; but even this is not a mere excrescence, for the observation of the Canaanites that 'This is a grievous mourning to the Egyptians' is an essential contribution to the colouring.

Now this is better than the Shipwrecked Sailor. Yet it is a passage not chosen for its unusual merit but taken entirely at random. And the Hebrew epic keeps up this admirable standard of story-telling throughout.

We now come to the most remarkable of the earlier Egyptian stories, the Tale of Sinuhe. It was composed early in the XIIth Dynasty, not long after 2000 B. C., and such was its popularity that 500 years later it was still being copied and studied in the writing schools.

It has no framework, and the story is told in the first person by its hero Sinuhe himself. He was returning from an expedition against the Libyans, commanded by the crown prince Senusret, when the king died. The news was brought to Senusret, who instantly left his army and made for the capital, evidently in order to make sure of the succession by his presence. The news, however, had also been conveyed independently to certain other princes who also were with the expedition, and overheard by Sinuhe, who, for reasons which he cannot wholly explain, even to himself—and this

is the point of the story—fled away secretly into Syria.
There he is well received by a chief, takes a wife and raises
a family, and fights in single combat with the leader of a
hostile confederation of Syrians. But at last homesickness
proves too strong for him and he longs to return to Egypt,
to serve the king, to whom he has been loyal throughout,
and above all to be buried in the land in which he was born.
The king hears of his distress, summons him back to Egypt,
pardons his flight, restores him to his position in the state,
and all ends happily.

Of this story Professor Gardiner, to whom we owe a
brilliant critical study and translation of it, writes as
follows:

'It will not be seriously contended that this story is one
of those world-masterpieces of literary skill which stand out
for all time as the perfect expression of some side of universal human experience or feeling. None the less I maintain that for us too the Story of Sinuhe is, and must remain,
a classic. It is a classic because it marks a definite stage in
the history of the world's literature; and it is a classic
because it displays with inimitable directness the mixed
naïveté and subtlety of the old Egyptian character, its
directness of vision, its pomposity, its reverence and its
humour. To those students of Ancient Egypt whose culture
is not of that narrow type that makes them insensible to
what is simple and unsophisticated, the vicissitudes of
Sinuhe's wanderings must be full of charm. There is plenty
of variety in these three hundred lines, the brief but lofty
description of the old king's death, the graphic narrative of
Sinuhe's flight; the terrors of the desert and the hospitality
of Beduin tribes; the adulatory but not unpoetic encomium
of Sesostris I. In the account of the duel with the mighty
man of Retenu we breathe the atmosphere of the Old
Testament, and the passage describing Sinuhe's longing
for Egypt is as perfect a revelation of Egyptian character
as may be found anywhere. Then there is Pharaoh's letter
of pardon, with its characteristic insistence on the all-

absorbing theme of burial rites, and Sinuhe's reply, in
which a very lively terror of the Pharaoh is blended with
a wholly artificial and calculated flattery. There is nothing
more vivid in the tale, I might almost say in *any* tale, than
the picture of Sinuhe's reception at Court. As by a magic
touch we are carried backward four thousand years to
witness Sinuhe's abject panic as he flings himself on the
ground at Pharaoh's feet, and to behold the tolerant *bon-
homie* of Pharaoh as he half-ironically introduces the dust-
stained warrior to the Queen; we can almost hear the
Queen's incredulous shriek of surprise, almost see the
twinkling feet of the little princesses as with dance and song
they plead that the stranger may be pardoned. The story
ends with the conventional description of an old age spent
amid luxury and honours, a description that serves to
remind us of the strongly materialistic bent of the Egyptians,
that love of good cheer and magnificence which is indeed
the key-note of the civilization of Ancient Egypt.' [1]

To my mind the interest of this story lies in its defects
almost more than in its virtues. It is the most Egyptian of
all the stories. Even the one universally human motif in it,
homesickness for the fatherland, is limited and Egyptianized
by the emphasis laid on a burial in Egyptian soil as the
most important consequence of the return. Two things,
however, are of vital importance. In the first place the
story is a psychological study, and in the second its very
artificiality both of construction and of style testifies to the
fact that Egyptian literature had already passed through
its apprenticeship, that style had become self-conscious, and
had already degenerated, in some cases at least, into an
overstraining after effect.

Let us take these two points in order. Sinuhe is a psychological study. The hero is constantly giving us his reasons

---

[1] Gardiner, *Notes on the Story of Sinuhe* (Paris, 1916), pp. 164–5. I
quote this in full, partly because it is in itself so admirable, and partly
because it is so rare for the commentator on an Egyptian document to
show any interest in or enthusiasm for its literary value.

for his actions and his attitude towards events. From himself and from others we learn in the course of the tale enough to sketch a fairly complete character of him; all we know about the mind of the Shipwrecked Sailor could be written in a dozen words. Most striking of all is Sinuhe's attitude to the flight itself. Why did he run away? many a reader has asked, and the answer is that he does not know himself. He gives us reasons, it is true. When he overhears the message being given to the princes, he says, *My heart became distraught, my arms spread apart, and trembling fell upon all my limbs. I leapt away from thence to seek a hiding-place. I crouched between two bushes to hide myself from the road and from him who fared upon it. I set out southward, though I purposed not to approach the capital, for I thought there would be strife and I had no mind to live after him* (i.e. the crown prince). Later he writes to the king, *As touching this flight, I planned it not, it was not in my heart, nor did I conceive it, I know not what drew me from the spot. It was like unto a dream, as when a man of the Delta finds himself in Elephantine, or a man of the marshes in Nubia.* And yet this is a warrior, loyal throughout to the prince whom he thus deserted, Sinuhe, the hero of a single combat with a mighty adversary in Syria. Surely there is real tragedy in this. The weak spot in the character of Hamlet the soldier led to five deaths in place of one, and Sinuhe's lack of resolution at this crisis also led to tragedy, the spending of the best years of his life abroad, and almost to the worst tragedy of all, burial in a foreign land.

And now for the second point, the artificiality of the form and style. It is true that there is much straightforward narrative in Sinuhe, there is good description, and there are dramatic touches. Here is the description of his treatment by his Syrian host:

He placed me above his children and married me with his eldest daughter. He made me to choose for myself of his land, of the best that was his upon the border of a neighbouring country. It was a goodly land called Yaa. There were figs in it and grapes, and its wine was more abundant than its water. Plentiful was its honey, many were its olives. There was barley in it and spelt, and limitless cattle of every kind. Great also was that which fell to my lot by reason of the love vouchsafed me. He made me ruler of a tribe in the best of his country. Food was provided me for my daily fare, and wine for my daily portion, cooked meat and roast fowl, over and above the game of the desert, for they hunted and laid before me in addition to the quarry of my dogs. And there were made for me many dainties, and milk cooked in every way.

There are some good touches in the earlier narrative of his crossing the frontier between the Egyptian Delta and Syria:

I ferried over in a barge without rudder, with the help of a westerly breeze. . . . I reached the Wall of the Ruler, built to repel the Syrian and to keep in subjection the Beduin of the desert. I crouched low in a thicket lest the sentry on duty on the wall should see me. . . . The attack of thirst overtook me. I was parched, my throat burned, and I said, This is the taste of death. Yet I lifted up my heart and girded up my loins. Then I heard the lowing of cattle and beheld men of Syria.

Against these simple virtues, however, must be set more than one defect. Sinuhe cannot clap into't roundly, but must begin with a formal list of his offices in the royal harem.[1] At one point the whole action is held up while he delivers a metrical panegyric on the present king of Egypt, and exhorts his Syrian hearer to keep on good terms with him. When the moment of recall comes a long, bombastic and extravagant court document is blatantly inserted, and no attempt is made to weave it into the texture of the narrative. It is even brutally labelled *Copy of the decree which was brought to the humble servant concerning his return to Egypt,* and we are not even spared a copy of Sinuhe's acknowledgement

---

[1] If, however, as has been suggested, the story either is, or at least takes the form of, a biographical inscription from a tomb, this formal introduction is excusable.

of this decree, couched in terms only less stilted. After these interludes, which, be it noted, are of considerable length, Sinuhe returns to his narrative, which flows smoothly and uninterruptedly to its finish.

The style, as well as the construction, is artificial. Scholars have pointed out several phrases which even we, with our comparatively small knowledge of Egyptian words, can with confidence stamp as affected. The similes, too, are often exaggerated. *Nay*, says Sinuhe to his Asiatic host, when the mighty man of another tribe challenges him to combat, *Nay, it is envy because he sees me doing thy behest. Verily I am like a wandering bull in the midst of a strange herd, and the steer of those cattle charges him, a long-horned bull attacks him. Does a bull love fighting and shall then a stronger bull wish to sound the retreat through dread lest that one might equal him? If his heart be for fight let him speak his will.* This is heavy going, and we suspect it was little lighter for the Egyptians than for us.

Yet despite its defects it is a well told story, and the earliest to realize that vital quality of atmosphere of which we shall have more to say later.

The tendency towards artificiality which shows itself in so sinister a fashion in this narrative runs riot completely in another famous story, the Tale of the Eloquent Peasant.[1] This, again, is of Middle Kingdom date, and, like Sinuhe, it was highly appreciated in later times. A peasant from one of the oases goes down into Egypt to sell the products of his land, which he loads upon his donkeys. Arrived in Egypt he is robbed of his donkeys and their load by means of a trick by a rogue called Dhutnakht. The peasant thereupon goes off to the capital of the district to complain to Dhutnakht's overlord, Rensi by name. Rensi summons his council of nobles to deal with the case, but for reasons not stated withholds judgement. The peasant now appeals to Rensi in language

[1] See F. Vogelsang, *Kommentar zu den Klagen des Bauern* (forming Band 6 of K. Sethe, *Untersuchungen zur Geschichte und Altertumskunde Aegyptens*), Leipzig, 1913.

so eloquent that Rensi deems the case worthy of the notice of the king, who orders him to keep the peasant in suspense in the hope of further eloquence. This expectation is not deluded, for the peasant utters a further series of complaints, eight in number, of which the following is a fair specimen.

O high steward my lord, thou art Re, the lord of heaven, along with thy courtiers. The sustenance of all mankind is from thee, even like the inundation. Thou art the Nile that maketh the meadows green and the waste places habitable.

Punish the robber, take counsel for the poor. Become not a torrent against the petitioner. Take heed to the approach of eternity. Seek to live long, even as it is said The doing of justice is the breath of the nose. Mete out punishment to him that should be punished. So shall none equal thee in rectitude. Doth the hand-balance deflect? Do the scales weigh falsely? Doth Thoth show leniency? If so then do thou work mischief. Make thyself the peer of these three, and if the three show leniency then do thou also show leniency.

This extract is from one of the easier of the complaints. There are others in which the peasant's imagination shows itself in even more perverted and far-fetched imagery and symbolism than this. In fact we perceive that the whole story is but an excuse for a display of a type of artificial and inartistic verbosity which, for all its absurdity, must have appealed to a large audience among the educated in Egypt. It is the full development of what we saw in germ in the Shipwrecked Sailor, and flourishing, though well cut back, in Sinuhe. Yet the introductory narrative is the most perfectly told in Egyptian literature, and is worthy to be placed beside any passage in the Old Testament which has no more emotional content.

There was once a man called Khuanūp, a peasant of the Valley of Salt, and he had a wife whose name was Mary.

And this peasant said to his wife, Behold I go down into Egypt to bring thence food for my children. Go now, measure out for me the corn which is in the barn, even that which remains of last year's (?) corn.

And he measured out to her six gallons of corn. And this peasant said to his wife, Behold there remain twenty gallons of corn for food for thee and for thy children. Do thou make for me these six gallons of corn into bread and beer for every day of my journey.

So this peasant went down into Egypt, after that he had loaded his asses with rushes, reremt-*plants, natron, salt, sticks, leopard skins,*[1] *full measure of all the goodly products of the Valley of Salt.*

This incongruous juxtaposition of the simple and beautiful with the artificial and ugly is not without its significance for the history of Egyptian literature. It is not a primitive but an advanced stage in story-writing. All the evidence in our possession goes to show that the high-water mark of Egyptian science and art was reached in the Old Kingdom, between the IVth and VIth Dynasties. From that period certainly come the originals of the mathematical and medical papyri; the architecture of that era, if equalled, was never surpassed; and the sculpture and painting of later days are for the most part but a pale shadow of what was then done. We might have expected that the same conditions which produced the best work in one art should produce the best in another; and this seems to have been the case. The Egyptians of the Middle Kingdom themselves attributed the origins of their wisdom-literature to the famous sages of the Vth Dynasty, and we may hazard the opinion that the Old Kingdom also saw the full bloom of the art of story-telling, and that the artificiality and sophistication of the Middle Kingdom stories are signs of decay. Unfortunately no stories have survived from the Old Kingdom, but Sinuhe and the Eloquent Peasant are sure evidence that they must have existed. The didactic literature, which reached its highest development shortly after the fall of the Old Kingdom,

[1] I have taken the liberty of shortening the 'catalogue' (cf. p. 30), the more so as most of the products contained in it are unidentified.

seems to have reacted strongly on the short story, and the result is admirably summed up by the three Middle Kingdom stories which we have described; the Shipwrecked Sailor is almost untouched straightforward narrative, the Peasant is a piece of wisdom-literature with a story for setting, and Sinuhe shows the complete fusion of the two genres in a clever but artificial psychological story.

From the point of view of narrative the artificiality and subtlety of Sinuhe and the Peasant are clearly defects. At the same time their authors were practising a higher and more difficult art than that of the Shipwrecked Sailor, and to one who did not know the later history of Egyptian literature these works would seem to give promise of great things. But the stagnation so typical of things Egyptian set in, and the experiments tried in these works do not seem to have been followed up.

The art of telling a simple story, however, was not by any means lost. The New Empire has given us a group of three stories written in the popular language of the period, known to philologists as Late Egyptian. All three are straightforward folk-tales. The first, contained in the Westcar Papyrus,[1] recounts how King Kheops of the IVth Dynasty ordered his sons to tell each in turn a story about magicians. The first story is almost completely lost. The second, told by Prince Khephren, tells how a magician called Ubaoner punished an adulterous townsman by making a crocodile of wax which at the critical moment turned into a real crocodile. Prince Baufrē tells how the magician Zazaemonkh recovered a lost amulet of turquoise from the bed of a lake. A part of this story may be quoted as an example of the style of the document, and because of the interesting parallel, doubtless accidental, with the crossing of the Red Sea by the Israelites.

The king is being rowed on his lake by a crew of beautiful maidens, who ply each one oar, the time being set by two leaders or stroke-oars, one on each side of the boat.

[1] A. Erman, *Die Märchen des Papyrus Westcar*, Berlin, 1890.

Now one of the leaders caught her braided hair, and her fish-pendant[1] of new[2] turquoise fell into the water. And she stopped[3] and ceased rowing. And her side stopped and ceased rowing. Then said his majesty, Will ye not row then? And they said, Our leader has stopped and is not rowing. And his majesty said to her, Why art thou not rowing? She said, Because a fish-pendant of new turquoise has fallen into the water. . . . And he said, I will replace it for thee. But she said, I prefer mine own thing to one like it.

The king then perceives that this is a case for a magician; the chief lector-priest and magician Zazaemonkh is summoned, and the story of the pendant is told to him.

Then the chief lector-priest Zazaemonkh said his magic spell. And he laid one side of the water of the lake upon the other and found the fish-pendant lying on a potsherd. And he brought it and gave it to her that owned it. Now the water was twelve cubits deep at its middle, and it reached twenty-four cubits when it had been turned back. Then he said his magic spell, and brought the waters of the lake back to their place.

But his majesty spent the whole day in merrymaking with the entire royal house, and rewarded the chief lector-priest Zazaemonkh with all manner of good things.

The last of the princes, Hardedef, proposes to the king not to tell some magic deed of the past but to produce a living magician who shall perform wonders in the king's presence. And this actually happens, for the old man Dedi, brought by the prince, redeems his boast that he can replace the severed head of a goose or an ox, and make a lion follow him submissively. He then, in answer to a question by the king, foretells the fall of the royal line and the passing of the succession to the children of a high-priest of the Sun-god at Heliopolis, and gives a detailed account of their birth.

[1] Women, when accompanying a fishing expedition, often wore such a pendant for luck.

[2] New, and hence more valuable, for old turquoise loses its colour.

[3] Or 'was silent', i. e. ceased singing.

Here we have clearly a fragment of history which has passed into folk-tale.

The second story of the group is that contained in the D'Orbiney Papyrus[1] and known as the Tale of Two Brothers. The brothers are called Anubis and Bata, and the long inconsequent narrative conceals, according to some, a myth concerning the two gods who bear these names. The structure of the story is very weak, and it is clearly an attempt to combine into continuous narrative several disconnected episodes. It tells how the young Bata lived with his married elder brother Anubis, and helped him with his work in the fields. Anubis's wife, however, tempts Bata in vain and then falsely accuses him to her husband. Bata flies, with Anubis in pursuit, but is saved by the Sun-god, who interposes between the brothers a lake full of crocodiles. A parley ensues, in which Bata proves his innocence and announces his determination of going off to the Valley of the Cedar and of placing his heart upon a cedar tree. When Anubis becomes aware, by a certain sign, that something has happened to his brother he is to go and seek the heart and put it in water, whereupon Bata will come to life and take vengeance for the wrong done to him. So Anubis goes home and kills his wife, and Bata goes off to the Valley of the Cedar. Here the gods, pitying his loneliness, make a wife for him. A lock of this woman's hair is caught by the sea and carried to Egypt, where its sweet perfume excites the interest of Pharaoh, who sends to the Valley of the Cedar, brings off the woman and makes her his favourite. She now persuades him to send and cut down the cedar, and with the fall of the cedar and of his heart, which was on it, Bata ceases to live.

Anubis now experiences the sign which Bata had foretold, namely the frothing-over of a pot of beer which he was about to drink, and goes to the Valley of the Cedar to look for the heart. After some delay he finds it in the form of a fruit, and

[1] *Select Papyri from the collections of the British Museum* (London, 1860), Part II, Pls. ix–xix.

Bata is brought to life again. He becomes a bull, and carries his brother on his back into Egypt, where he reveals his identity to his faithless wife. She persuades Pharaoh to sacrifice the bull, which he does; but two persea trees grow up where two drops of his blood touch the ground, and in these Bata still lives. He again reveals himself to his wife, who persuades Pharaoh to cut down the trees and make them into furniture. In the cutting, however, a splinter enters the mouth of the wife and she conceives a son, who is made crown prince. On the death of the king this child, who is none other than Bata himself, succeeds to the throne and at last takes vengeance on the wife.

This story is exceedingly well told, as all who read the extracts now to be given will agree. It has attained a somewhat undeserved notoriety owing to the suggestion more than once made, but difficult to justify, that the episode of Bata and the wife of Anubis is the origin of the story of Joseph and Potiphar's wife. For this reason it may be of interest if we choose our quotations from the part of the story which deals with this incident.

Now many days after this they were in the field and they were short of seed. And he sent his younger brother saying, Go fetch us seed from the village. And his younger brother found his elder brother's wife sitting at her hair-dressing. And he said to her, Arise and give me seed, that I may go to the field, for my elder brother is waiting for me. Make no delay. And she said to him, Go, open the bin and take for thyself what thou willst; make me not leave my hair-dressing in the midst.

So the youth went into his stall and brought forth a great vessel, being minded to take away much seed. And he loaded himself with barley and spelt and went out with it. And she said to him, How much is that which is upon thy shoulder? And he said to her, Three bushels of spelt and two bushels of barley, five in all, is what is upon my shoulder. So said he to her. And she conversed with him, saying, Verily great might is in thee, for I behold thy strength daily. For her desire was to know him in the knowledge of youth. And she arose

*and seized hold of him and said, Come let us spend an hour of love.
It shall profit thee, for I will make thee fine raiment. But the youth
became like a panther in rage at this wicked thing which she had said
to him, so that she was sore afraid. And he spake unto her saying,
Lo, thou art unto me as a mother, and thy husband is to me as a father,
for he is older than I and hath brought me up. What is this great
abomination which thou hast spoken? Say it not again unto me. I
will tell it to no man, and will not suffer it to come forth from my
mouth to any man. And he took up his load and went off into the
fields. And he came to his elder brother and they occupied themselves
with their work.*

*Now at eventide his elder brother ceased work and went home to his
house, but his younger brother tended his cattle and loaded himself
with all manner of products of the field. And he drove his cattle
before him in order to let them sleep in their stall in the village.*

*But the wife of his elder brother was afraid by reason of what she
had said. So she took fat and grease and feigned to have been beaten,
that she might say to her husband, It is thy younger brother that has
beaten me. And the husband came home in the evening as his daily
wont was. He came to his house and found his wife lying feigning to
be sick: she poured no water on his hands as was her wont, and she
had lighted no light against his return, and his house was in darkness.
And she lay there vomiting. And her husband said to her, Who hath
spoken with thee? And she said unto him, No man hath spoken with
me save thy younger brother. When he came to take the seed and
found me sitting alone he said to me, Come let us pass an hour of love.
Cover thy hair. So said he to me, but I heeded not. I said to him, Lo,
am I not thy mother, and is not thy elder brother unto thee as a father?
And he was afraid and beat me, that I might not tell it to thee. If
therefore thou suffer him to live I shall die forthwith. Behold, when
he cometh home in the evening ⟨thou shalt kill him⟩, for I abhor this
evil thing that he would have done yesterday.*[1]

*Then his elder brother became even as a panther. He made sharp
his spear and took it in his hand. So his elder brother was standing
behind the door of his stall to slay his younger brother at his coming
in the evening to put his cattle into the stall.*

[1] Note that with sunset a new day has begun.

And when the sun set he loaded himself with all manner of herbs of the field as was his daily wont. And he returned home. And as the first cow was entering the stall she said unto her herdsman, Behold, thy elder brother standeth waiting for thee with his spear to slay thee. Flee from him. And he understood what his first cow said. And as the next entered she said likewise. And he looked under the door of his stall and he saw the feet of his elder brother as he stood behind the door with his spear in his hand. And he laid his load down on the ground and betook himself to flight.

The third story is contained in a papyrus known as Harris 500.[1] It is called the Story of the Foredoomed Prince. It contains two main ideas, that of a prince who is foredoomed to die by a snake, a crocodile or a dog, and that of a princess imprisoned by her father in a lofty tower and offered in marriage to him who shall first climb to her window. It begins very simply as follows:

They say there was once a king who had no son. He begged for himself a son from the gods of his time, and they decreed that one should be born to him. Now that night he slept with his wife, and his wife conceived. And when she had fulfilled the months of childbirth a son was born. The Hathors came to decree for him a destiny. They said, He shall die by the crocodile, the snake or the dog. And the people who were about the child heard it and told it to his majesty. Then his majesty became exceeding sore at heart. And his majesty caused to be built for him a house of stone on the desert, equipped with servants and with every good thing pertaining to a royal house, and the child was not to go outside it.

Now when the child grew up he went on to his roof and saw a greyhound following a man who was walking on the road. And he said to his attendant who was beside him, What is that which is following the man who is coming along the road? And he said to him, It is a dog. Then the child said to him, Let there be brought to me one like it. And the attendant went and told it to his majesty. His

---

[1] *Egyptian Hieratic Papyri in the British Museum*, 2nd series, 1923, Pls. xlviii-lii.

majesty said, Let a little puppy be taken to him lest his heart be grieved. So they took him the dog.

With this begin the adventures. The prince wearies of life in his castle and goes off to Naharin,[1] where he finds the young nobles of the country essaying to win the chief's daughter by climbing to her window. He joins in the contest, is successful, and marries the princess. With their married life the prophecy begins to work itself out, for a first attempt on the prince's life is made by the snake, who, however, is defeated by the watchfulness of the wife. The end of the papyrus is damaged, and the fragmentary remains show us the crocodile and the dog both in action, not to mention a water-spirit. Which of the two animals eventually causes the death of the hero we cannot say.

These three stories are simple folk-tales admirably told. There is no characterization in them, no psychological interest, and their literary value—for they have one—lies in their simplicity, their choice of common words, and the directness of their method.

One more story from the New Kingdom must not go unnoticed, for it differs considerably from these in style, and indeed is our only evidence that the subtler art of storytelling shown in Sinuhe had not altogether perished with the XIIth Dynasty. It is the Story of Wenamun,[2] and takes the form of a report submitted to the king, probably the last Ramesses, about 1100 B.C., by an official who had been sent to Syria to fetch wood for the sacred barge of Amun. Some have even held that it is an historical document; if so it is by far the most vivid that has come down to us.

Wenamun leaves the court at Thebes and arrives at Tanis in the Delta, where he has to beg a safe-conduct and a ship from Smendes, the king of the rival dynasty which had established itself in Lower Egypt.

I remained in Tanis until the fourth month of summer. Smendes

---

[1] North-east of Syria.
[2] From a papyrus in Moscow. See *Zeitschr. f. äg. Sprache*, xxxviii, pp. 1 ff.

*and Thentamun[1] sent me forth with the ship-captain Mengebet, and
on the first day of the fourth month of summer I went down to the
Great Syrian Sea. I came to Dor, a city of Zakar, and its prince
Beder sent to me fifty loaves, one mesekh of wine and the leg of an ox.
Then a man of my ship fled, taking gold [vessels amounting to]
5 deben, four silver theb-vessels, making 20 deben, and a bag of
silver value 11 deben; total [of what he stole], 5 deben of gold and
31 deben of silver.*

Wenamun now tries to persuade the prince of Dor to
recover his money for him. But at the end of nine days
nothing has been done and he thereupon quarrels with the
prince of Dor and sails to Byblos[2], where he receives a
very half-hearted welcome from the chief.

*I passed nineteen days in his harbour, and he continued sending to
me daily saying, Get thee out of my harbour. Now as he was offering
to his gods the god took possession of one of his elder children and
made him rave; and he cried, Bring up the god,[3] bring the envoy that
beareth him. It is Amun that sent him, it is he that caused him to
come.*

*So raved the frenzied one in that night. But I had found a ship[4]
that was bound for Egypt, and had loaded all that I had upon her and
was watching for darkness, thinking that when it fell I would
embark the god so that no other eye might see him. And the harbour-
master came to me, saying, The prince bids thee abide until morning.
And I said to him, Art thou not he that did come to me daily saying,
Get thee out of my harbour? Surely thou wilt not now bid me abide,
that the ship which I have found may put out and thou mayest then
again come and say, Get thee gone? And he went and told it to the
prince. And the prince sent to the captain of the ship saying, The*

[1] Thentamun is presumably the wife of Smendes.

[2] I have assumed that Erman is right in placing here the fragment
of the papyrus numbered III.

[3] On arriving at Byblos, Wenamun had disembarked the statue of
Amun which had been sent with him to ensure the success of his
expedition and concealed it in a cave.

[4] Wenamun had by this time lost touch with the boat which had
been lent to him by Smendes.

prince bids thee abide until tomorrow. And when the morrow came he sent and brought me up; but the god rested in the cave wherein he was, by the edge of the sea. Now I found him sitting in his upper chamber, his back leaning against a balcony, and the waves of the Syrian Sea beating behind him. I said to him, May Amun be gracious. And he said to me, How long is it since the day when thou camest from the place wherein Amun dwells? And I answered him, It is five whole months.

The prince now reproaches Wenamun with his inability to produce his papers of recommendation, and reminds him that though his predecessors provided cedar at Amun's request they did so in return for an adequate present, and he even produces his account-books to prove this statement. Wenamun thereupon sends to Smendes to borrow more money. On receiving this the prince of Byblos releases the wood, and Wenamun is about to sail off, when eleven ships belonging to his enemies of Zakar are sighted, their orders being to take him prisoner. The prince of Byblos, however, refuses to give him up. *I cannot take prisoner the envoy of Amun in my own land,* he says, *but let me dispatch him and ye may pursue him and imprison him.* So Wenamun is sent off; but the men of Zakar do not catch him, for the wind drives him to Alashiya, probably a small kingdom in the extreme north of Syria. Here the people would have killed him, but he was saved by an appeal to the queen. The rest of his adventures here are lost, and we do not know how he got back to Egypt to make his report.

This story is an important piece of literature. It stands out in worth against the background of the simple folk-tales of the New Kingdom just as strongly as Sinuhe in the Middle Kingdom stands out against the Shipwrecked Sailor. Vivid description and pointed conversation are its more obvious merits, but its greatest qualities lie in its production of atmosphere and in the psychological treatment of the chief character, Wenamun. He reveals his feelings and claims our sympathy. Times have

changed and the envoy of the effete XXth Dynasty can
no longer give his orders in the Lebanon. But how well
he tells his story! How clearly do we see the picture of his
interview with the prince of Byblos, who sits *in his upper
chamber, his back leaning against a balcony, and the waves of the
Syrian Sea beating behind him*! How we share his disgust when
one of his own ship's company goes off with most of his gold
and silver in the harbour of Dor; how we sympathize with
his discomfiture when he is unable to produce his papers of
recommendation, and with his despair when he sees the
birds migrate for the second time to Egypt, while he still
lingers in Syria, his mission unfulfilled! Here is a story which
has almost all the characteristics of great literature, and yet
there is no striving after effect. A wonderful picture is this
of the decline and fall of the Egyptian empire, impregnated
with a pathetic belief in the power of Amun to save as of old.
This is a story worthy to be set side by side with some of the
best things in the Old Testament, the story of Jonah and his
mission, or that of Ruth amid the alien corn. Let us not
forget that it is five centuries earlier than either.

LECTURE II

THOUGH it so happens that, for us moderns at all events, the origin of drama lies rather in an unessential embellishment of a religious dance than in a direct and natural development of the short story or the epic, yet in its early forms it has strong affinities with the latter, and it seems therefore not unreasonable to deal with it at this stage of our enquiry.

Herodotus [1] gives us descriptions of Egyptian religious festivals in which numbers of people seem to be re-enacting some scene in the lives of the gods. The gravestone of a certain Ikhernofret [2] of the XIIth Dynasty from Abydos tells how this nobleman was sent by his king to Abydos to restore the temple, and how he there performed certain mysteries connected with the death of Osiris, mysteries clearly, from their description, of a dramatic or at least pantomimic nature. It has long been known, too, that a much-worn stone in the British Museum preserves portions of a mime connected with the story of Osiris, but it has only recently been shown that in this text, which in origin goes back at least to the Old Kingdom, we have the actual dialogue of the actors, who represent various gods and goddesses, together with stage directions, and also a narrative interspersed between the speeches of the characters by a reciter who performed much the same function as the captions of a cinematograph film.[3] Still more recently a papyrus has been published which shows that the ceremonies connected with the coronation of the king were in part of a similar dramatic nature.[4] Since the king is the earthly representative of the god Horus, and the dead king

[1] ii, 60 ff.

[2] Schäfer, H., *Die Mysterien des Osiris in Abydos*, in Kurt Sethe, *Untersuchungen zur Geschichte und Altertumskunde Aegyptens*, Band IV.

[3] Sethe, K., *Dramatische Texte zu altaegyptischen Mysterienspielen*, i, in *Untersuchungen* etc., Band X, 1.

[4] Sethe, K., *op. cit.*, ii, in *Untersuchungen*, etc., Band X, 2.

is identified with Osiris, it is natural that here too the myth of Osiris should be the source from which the scenes are drawn, but here, from the very nature of the case, the actors, who are the king, his children, and others concerned in the coronation, do not sink their earthly personalities quite so completely as the actors in the scenes described above.[1]

From the literary point of view this amounts to very little, for it merely indicates that there was, in connexion with religious ceremonies in Egypt, some kind of dramatic representation comparable perhaps with the more primitive European Mystery Plays of the Middle Ages. At the same time there is no sign that this ever underwent any serious development or gave place to drama in the true sense of the word.

Curiously enough attention has recently been drawn to the possible existence of a similar dramatic element in Babylonian religion.[2] A very obscure text dealt with by Zimmern seems to show that certain religious myths were enacted in pantomime, without any accompanying text, a singer being employed to fill in the intervals between the scenes. Some of the incantation texts, too, contain dialogue of a type which suggests that the ritual of incantation was in part pantomimic. Here again, however, all is very primitive.

Among the Hebrews there is no evidence of the existence of anything of this kind. Some commentators have, it is true, attempted to show that the Song of Solomon is a dramatic composition, but their reasons are not very convincing, and the name dramatic lyric, in the sense in which Browning uses it, seems far more suitable to the work. The same title might with equal justice be applied, in spite of its length, to the Book of Job.

---

[1] Yet another dramatic text has recently been published by Drioton, *Une scène des mystères d'Horus* in *Revue de l'Égypte ancienne*, ii, pp. 172 ff.

[2] Weber, *Lit.*, pp. 32–3; Zimmern, *Mittheilungen der Vorderasiatischen Gesellschaft*, iii, p. 16.

On present evidence it would seem that none of these early nations passed beyond the most elementary stage in the development of drama, and it was reserved for a people of greater artistic genius out of much the same origins to create drama in the full sense of the word. Thespis and his rout need not fear for their laurels.

By lyric compositions I mean those which show some sort of metrical structure, which are comparatively short in length, and which are primarily intended to be recited or sung. Such works are represented in the ancient world by hymns and psalms addressed to gods and kings, prayers, incantations, more rarely by secular poems and in particular love-songs.

The fact that these compositions should have taken metrical form in all three countries gives us pause at the outset, and indeed some have been tempted to assume a single place of origin, or at any rate to attribute the occurrence of verse in Hebrew literature to the influence of either Egyptian or Babylonian. This is probably unnecessary. There seems to be a tendency for some kind of metrical arrangement to develop very early in any literature, showing itself almost invariably in songs and hymns, where it may be in some sense dependent on music or dance rhythms, and sometimes in epic, as in Babylonia and Greece. Let us not forget the paradoxical truth that the literature of a people may be comparatively highly developed long before the introduction of writing. There are lyrics in the Old Testament which are much older than the prose settings in which we find them, and some of them may well precede the introduction of writing into Palestine, though the date of this is a question which I here purposely avoid. However this may be, it is certain that literature never waited upon writing.

Now such a pre-writing literature, if I may so call it, must have been dependent for its existence and preservation on recitation, and recitation is a matter of memory. We know ourselves that verse is more easily remembered than prose, and it may be that some process of natural selection came into play, which enabled those things to be most easily preserved which possessed, if only by accident, some elements of symmetry and balance. These qualities would in time come to be regarded as ends desirable in themselves, and this primitive unwritten literature would tend to fall into forms which possessed this kind of regularity. It showed itself, however, not only in the form of metre but in the form of parallelism both of words and meaning. This last is indeed a feature both of Babylonian and of Egyptian lyrics, but it is still more strongly characteristic of Hebrew, where, in such books as the Psalms and the Proverbs, it is carried so far that it tends to become cloying. Hebrew never outlived this form, as Egyptian did, and her failure to do so may be reckoned to her as a defect. Modern poetry, while tending to preserve and to develop metre, has almost completely abandoned parallelism of word and meaning, and has gained thereby, though the device is still occasionally used with wonderful effect:

> *Peace, come away, the song of woe*
> *Is after all an earthly song.*
> *Peace, come away, we do him wrong*
> *To sing so wildly. Let us go.*

The metrical forms of Hebrew poetry have been carefully studied, and I need only refer you to Dr. George Adam Smith's Schweich Lectures for 1910.[1]

In Babylonian, as in Hebrew, we find a division into lines, each of which may be separated into two half-lines, each containing a fixed number of stress accents.[2] The lines group themselves into strophes containing most commonly two pairs of lines, or half-strophes containing only one pair. Each line contains a complete sentence and each strophe a complete unit of thought.

[1] *The Early Poetry of Israel*, pp. 11 ff.

[2] Weber, *Lit.*, pp. 35–7, and references there given.

The exact structure of the versification which undoubtedly exists in most Egyptian lyrics is difficult to determine,[1] partly because in many manuscripts the red dots which normally mark the ends of the separate lines have been omitted by the scribe, partly because of the absence of vowels and the variable writing of the consonants. At the same time a strophic arrangement is sometimes quite obvious, consisting generally of groups of three or four connected lines, each group often beginning with the same word. This strophic arrangement may be accompanied by parallelism of meaning, though this element does not play as great a part in Egyptian as in Hebrew lyrics. When we come, however, to analyze the metre of the separate lines

[1] On this point see Erman, *Hymnen an das Diadem der Pharaonen* (*Abhandl. der. Kgl. Akad. d. Wiss.*, Phil.-hist. Klasse, Berlin, 1911), pp. 15 ff.; also Erman, *Lit.*, pp. 9 ff. (transl. Blackman, pp. xxx ff.). In the latter passage Erman says, 'Everything that the Egyptian writes in poetical language falls into short lines of approximately equal length, and, although we know nothing about their sound, it is natural to us to regard these lines as verses, that is to say, to attribute to them a metrical structure. This is doubtless right in many cases, certainly in those where a fixed number of lines, generally three or four, is grouped together according to the sense:

> *Thou embarkest in a ship of cedar wood,*
> *Manned from stem to stern,*
> *And farest to this thy beauteous castle*
> *Which thou hast builded for thyself.*
>
> *Thy mouth is filled with wine and beer*
> *And bread and meat and cakes:*
> *Oxen are slain and wine-jars broached,*
> *And pleasant song is before thee.*
>
> *Thy chief anointer anoints with kemi-oil,*
> *Thy head gardener brings garlands;*
> *The overseer of thy serfs offers birds*
> *And thy fisherman fish.*

These are certainly verses.'

we find ourselves in difficulties. Though there seems good reason to believe that every Egyptian word had one strongly accented vowel, and that this vowel was long if in an open syllable and short if in a closed syllable, yet we do not know enough about the vocalization of words in general to make much use of this knowledge.[1] In the Coptic poetry of a much later period each line seems to have had from two to four accents, with varying numbers of unaccented or weakly accented syllables in between. This gives rise to what may be described as a free rhythm rather than a strict metre. It is probable that the versification of much of the ancient Egyptian lyric poetry was of a similar loose nature.

In this connexion Erman has shown that in the short oft-repeated verses of the hymns the simple name of the god or king is often lengthened by the addition of epithets, or replaced by a long periphrasis which would totally destroy the metre of the line if this were at all strict. Thus in the very common morning hymn which runs: [2]

1. eryáseth em hátep   *Thou wakest in peace;*
2. eryás Menháyet em hátep *Menhayet awaketh in peace.*
3. reswáteth hetáptey   *May thy awakening be peaceful.*

the name of the goddess Menhāyet is, in versions of this hymn addressed to various other gods, replaced by names and titles which instead of one accent have as many as eight or nine. Such lyrics could only be sung or recited in a style which allowed great freedom between the fixed points of the lines, a style perhaps not unlike that used for the singing of psalms and canticles in our English churches to-day, where the inconveniently long phrases are dealt with by

---

[1] See H. Junker, *Poesie aus der Spätzeit*, in *Zeitschr. für ägyptische Sprache*, xliii, pp. 101 ff. The verses there published have from two to four accents to the line.

[2] The vowels used are mainly fictitious as regards quality. As regards quantity the only long vowels are probably those so marked. The sign ′ indicates the stress accent.

crowding a large number of syllables on to a single note of the tune.

An odd element in Egyptian lyric poetry, for which it is difficult to feel much enthusiasm, is the literary device of playing upon words. The Egyptian was an inveterate punster, and he would have been ungrateful had he not been, for the development of the Egyptian script out of a series of mere picture-drawings was based on the pun.[1] Thus the vanquished land of Syria (*kharew*) is said to have been 'made a widow' (*khare*) by reason of Egypt.[2] A Hymn to Amun from a papyrus now in Leyden [3] is divided into numbered chapters each of which begins with a pun on its number in the series; what is worse, the numbers are not all consecutive, but are chosen according to their adaptability to punning.

Rhyme, which plays a not very large role in Hebrew poetry and probably none at all in Babylonian, has not so far been detected in Egyptian.

The contribution made by the Hebrews to the lyrics of the world is very great. Not only have we the early songs scattered through the great national epic, but we have the books of Psalms, Proverbs and Ecclesiastes, and the superb love-poem known as the Song of Solomon. Babylonia too has given her share in this kind. Her prayers and her psalms, particularly those of the penitential type, form a mass of valuable literature.

[1] Thus the picture of a draught-board (?) with its men, originally used only to write that object itself, whose name was pronounced approximately *māne*, also served to write the abstract verb 'to remain', one of whose commonest parts had the same sound. Without some such punning transference Egyptian writing could never have passed beyond the stage of elementary picture-writing.

[2] On the so-called Israel-stela of Merenptah.

[3] See A. H. Gardiner, *Hymns to Amon from a Leyden Papyrus* in *Zeitschr. für ägyptische Sprache*, xlii, pp. 12 ff. Chapter 6, for example, begins, *Every region is full of thy fear*, where the word for 'region', approximately *sŏw*, is a pun on the numeral 6, which had the same sound.

What has Egypt to offer us in this genre? On the tomb-walls of the Egyptian noblemen scenes are not uncommon in which singing, often to the accompaniment of a flute or harp, or both, is represented. It is clear that singing played a great part both in everyday life and in religious services. Singing demands songs, and fortunately many of these have come down to us, both secular and religious.

Of the former many have in themselves but little value. That sung by the herdsman to his oxen as they tread the corn runs as follows:

> *Thresh for yourselves, thresh for yourselves, ye oxen.*
> *Thresh for yourselves, thresh for yourselves.*
> *Straw for to eat, and barley for your masters.*
> *Let not your hearts grow faint, for one is yet cool*(?).

This is not great poetry. But the Egyptian can do far better than this. Here is a song which was written up in several tombs beside the picture of a harper, and which evidently enjoyed a long vogue in Egypt.[1] It breathes the spirit of *carpe diem*, a phrase indeed to which Egyptian possessed a close analogy in the common phrase *irt hrw nfr*, 'to make a happy day ', i. e. 'to enjoy oneself'.

> *It is well*(?) *with this noble prince. The happy destiny hath come*
>   *to pass.*
> *Generations pass away and others stand in their place since the*
>   *time of them that were of old.*
> *Re getteth him up in the morning and Atum*[2] *setteth in the west.*
> *Men beget, women conceive, and every nose draweth breath,*
> *But when day dawneth their children are come in their place.*

---

[1] Preserved in Pap. Harris 500, recto, 6.2. ff.; it is there stated to have been taken from the tomb of King Antef, where it stood in front of the figure of a harper. There is also a copy in the tomb of Neferhotep at Thebes (Max Müller, *Die Liebespoesie der alten Ägypter*, Tafel I). Both texts are very difficult and probably corrupt. The translation here offered is a free version of a combination of the two.

See too, for another such song, A. H. Gardiner in *Proc. Soc. Bibl. Arch.*, xxxv, 165 ff.   [2] Another name for Re, the Sun-god.

*The gods that were aforetime rest in their pyramids, likewise the
noble and the glorified, buried in their pyramids.*

*They that built them castles, their places are no more. What hath
become of them?*

I have heard the discourses of Imhotep and Hardedef [1] *with whose
words men speak everywhere(?).*

*Where are their places now? Their walls are destroyed, their
habitations are destroyed as if they had never been.*

*None cometh again from thence that he may tell us of their state,
that he may recount to us their lot, that he may set our heart at
rest(?) until we also hasten away to the place whither they are
gone.*

*Rejoice, and let thy heart forget that day when they shall lay thee
to rest.*

*Cast all sorrow behind thee, and bethink thee of joy until there
come that day of reaching port in the land that loveth silence.*

*Follow thy desire as long as thou livest, put myrrh on thy head,
clothe thee in fine linen.*

Set singing and music before thy face.

*Increase yet more the delights which thou hast, and let ⟨not⟩ thy
heart grow faint. Follow thine inclination and thy profit(?).
Do thy desires upon earth, and trouble not thine heart until that
day of lamentation come to thee.*

*Spend a happy day and weary not thereof. Lo, none may take his
goods with him, and none that hath gone may come again.*

This is clearly a poem of very considerable merit, and it
will hardly be supposed that this standard was reached
without a long and painful apprenticeship. Some traces of
this have survived.

The earliest date from the Old Kingdom, and are to be
found mainly in the so-called Pyramid Texts, which,
except for the biographies of a few nobles inscribed in
their tombs, are almost all the literature of that epoch
which has directly survived. 'Pyramid Texts' is the name
given to the mass of inscribed material which has been

---

[1] Wise men of old.

recovered from the walls of the inner chambers of the Vth and VIth Dynasty pyramids. It is wholly funerary in character, and consists mainly of magic spells designed to assist the dead kings in avoiding the endless terrors with which the morbid Egyptian imagination had filled the life to come.

The literary value of this material is not very high, yet it is sufficient to show us that as early as the Vth Dynasty [1] the Egyptians possessed a certain power of imaginative writing which is not without its effect. The passage which best illustrates this has often been quoted under the title of the Cannibal Hymn.[2] Here, in accordance with a primitive conception of heaven, the dead king Unas is described as hunting, slaying and devouring the gods.

The sky rains, the stars are darkened:
The Bows are in commotion, the bones of the Earth-gods tremble.
The Pleiades are silent when they behold Unas going up, a soul,
As a god who lives on his fathers and feeds on his mothers.
Unas is a lord of judgement(?), whose name his mother knows
  not.
The glory of Unas is in heaven, his might is in the horizon.
Even as his father Atum, who begat him. Yea, he begat Unas, but
  Unas is mightier than he.
The kas of Unas are about him and his qualities are beneath his
  feet.
His gods are upon him and his protecting serpents are upon his
  forehead.
The Serpent who leads Unas is before him, even she who beholds
  the external form(?), Spirit of flame.
The might of Unas protects him.
Unas is the bull of heaven, thrusting(?) with his desire, living
  upon the being of every god.

[1] And probably earlier, for many of the spells were undoubtedly old when they were inscribed in the pyramids.

[2] For a valuable study of this text see R. O. Faulkner in *Journal of Egyptian Archaeology*, x, pp. 97 ff.

Who eats their organs(?), who comes when their bodies are filled
    with magic
From the Island of Flame.
Unas is equipped, his spirits are united.
Unas is gone up as that great one, a possessor of subordinates.
He sitteth with his back to the Earth-god.
It is Unas that judgeth along with him whose name is hidden,
On that day of slaughtering the eldest.
Unas is lord of offerings, who knots the rope,
Who makes his meals for himself.
Unas eats men and lives upon gods;
A possessor of messengers who sends forth behests.
It is the Seizer of Horns who is in Kehau who lassoes them for
    Unas.
It is the Erect of Head who guards them for him, who holds them
    back for him.
It is He who is upon the Willows(?) who binds them for him.
It is the Wanderer who Slaughters Lords who strangles(?) them
    for him.
He draws forth their entrails for him.
The messenger he, whom he sends to punish.
It is He of the Wine-press who slays them for Unas,
Who cooks for him a meal thereof in his supper kettles.
Unas devours their magic, he swallows their spirits.
Their great ones are for his morning meal,
Their middle-sized ones are for his afternoon meal,
Their little ones are for his evening meal.
Their old men and old women are for his censings.
It is the Great Ones in the north of heaven who lay for him a fire
Of the thighs of their oldest to the kettles that contain them.
They who are in heaven fetch and carry for Unas.
The cooking pots are cleaned out(?) for him with the thighs of their
    women.
He has encircled the Two Heavens in their entirety, he has en-
    compassed the Two Banks.
Unas is a Great Mighty One who has power over great mighty
    ones.

Unas is a divinity, most divine of the great divinities(?).
Him whom he finds in his path, he eats him raw.
The protection of Unas is in front of all the noble ones who are in the horizon.
Unas is a god, older than the oldest.
Thousands serve him, hundreds make offering to him.
There has been given to him a writing of appointment as a Great Mighty One by Orion, father of the gods.
Unas has appeared again in heaven, he is crowned Lord of the Horizon.
He has broken their joints and their vertebrae.
He has taken away the hearts of the gods.
He has eaten the Red Crown, he has swallowed the Green Crown.
Unas feeds on the lungs of the Wise Ones.
He delights in living on hearts and on their magic too.
Unas rejoices(??) when he devours the śbšw that are in the Red Crown.
He flourishes, for their magic is in his belly.
The dignities of Unas cannot be taken away from him.
He has swallowed the intelligence of every god.
The lifetime of Unas is eternity, his duration is everlasting,
In this his prerogative of doing what he would and doing not that which he would not,
On the bounds of the horizon for ever and ever.
Behold their form is in the belly of Unas, their spirits are with Unas,
As his superfluity of food over and above the gods. Unas's burnt offering(?) consists of their bones.
Lo, their form is with Unas, their shadows are in the hand of their companions(?).
Unas is among them(?), a riser who rises(?), a hidden one who is hidden(?).
The doers of evil deeds have no power to hack up the earth.
The favourite place of Unas is among them who dwell in this earth for ever and ever.

The artistic value of this work is very slight. The subject

is ghoulish and unsympathetic, and its treatment chaotic.
The description of the cannibal feast of the dead king is
constantly interrupted by phrases which have nothing to
do with it and merely contain some obscure mythological
reference to his power or qualities. Even the incidents of
the feast itself are presented in very disorderly fashion. One
is almost tempted to suspect that the whole consists of short
quotations taken alternately from two separate hymns, one
describing the feast and the other praising the dead
king.

It is not possible to say whether there is any metrical
arrangement in the passage. Parallelism of syntax and of
meaning is, however, a very strong element in it. This
phenomenon is characteristic of the Pyramid Texts, and
occurs there both in its crudest form, which consists of the
constant repetition of a sentence, with only one word, generally its subject or object, changed, and in the more highly
developed form which we have in the Cannibal Hymn.[1]
The contemporary appearance of two widely separated
stages in the development of this kind of writing is probably
to be explained by the supposition that these texts contain
material of different dates. Sethe's recent masterly treatment of the dramatic texts mentioned above in any case
increases the probability that much of this material is considerably older than the date at which it was inscribed in
the pyramids, and we should be very unwise to assume
that anything in it is fairly representative of the lyrics of the
Vth and VIth Dynasties.

Apart from the hymns embodied in the Pyramid Texts
only one Old Kingdom group has survived, namely those
collected in a papyrus now in the Museum in Moscow.[2]
They are addressed to the royal crown of Egypt under its
various names; the wearer of the crown, however, is not the
King, as it must have been in the original form of the

[1] See Faulkner, *op. cit.*, pp. 100–102.

[2] Erman, *Hymnen an das Diadem der Pharaonen*, in *Abhandlungen der Kgl.
Preuss. Akademie der Wissenschaften*, phil.-hist. Klasse, 1911. Berlin, 1911.

hymns, but the god Sobk, to whom they thus have, as it were, a secondary dedication. They depend for their effect mainly upon somewhat crude parallelism of members.

Two examples are here quoted, addressed respectively to the White Crown of Upper, and to the Red Crown of Lower Egypt:

Adoration of the White Crown.[1]

Hail to thee, Eye of Horus, white and great,
  In whose beauty the Nine Gods rejoice
  When it rises on the eastern horizon.
They whom the Sky-god upholds(?) praise thee,
  Who sink in the western horizon,
  When thou art made to shine bright for them that are in the
    Underworld.
Grant that Sobk may conquer the Two Lands by thy might.
  Grant that he may rule over them.
Grant that mankind may come to him bowing the knee, even to
    Sobk,
  For thou art the Mistress of Diadems.[2]

Adoration of the Red Crown.[3]

The Red Crown gleams upon thee, O Sobk, that thou mayest be
  protected.[4]
The Red Crown towers high upon thee, that thou mayest be pro-
  tected.
Its spiral [5] is in front of thee, that thou mayest be protected.
Its sides are upon thy temples, that thou mayest be protected.

---

[1] Erman, *op. cit.*, p. 22.

[2] There is strophic arrangement here, two strophes of three lines each being followed by two strophes each of two; in the latter, however, the metre is thrown out by the insertion of a long name (here omitted) for the god Sobk in place of an original shorter word for the king.

[3] Erman, *op. cit.*, p. 46.

[4] The protective powers of the two royal crowns of Egypt is a commonplace of Egyptian literature.

[5] The Red Crown had, attached to its centre, a spiral which projected in front.

O all ye gods, of the south, of the north, of the west, of the east,
Who are in the following of Sobk,
Your souls shall rejoice in this King of Lower Egypt, even Sobk,
As Isis rejoiced in her son Horus the child in Khemmis.[1]

Compare with these the theophany of 2 Samuel xxii, which I choose because in subject matter it has some superficial affinities with the Cannibal Hymn:

Then the earth shook and trembled; the foundations of heaven moved and shook, because he was wroth.

There went up a smoke out of his nostrils, and fire out of his mouth devoured: coals were kindled by it.

He bowed the heavens also, and came down; and darkness was under his feet.

And he rode upon a cherub, and did fly: and he was seen upon the wings of the wind.

And he made darkness pavilions round about him, dark waters, and thick clouds of the skies.

Through the brightness before him were coals of fire kindled.

The Lord thundered from heaven, and the most High uttered his voice.

And he sent out arrows, and scattered them; lightning, and discomfited them.

And the channels of the sea appeared, the foundations of the world were discovered, at the rebuking of the Lord, at the blast of the breath of his nostrils.

Here is poetry beside which the Egyptian lyrics are not worthy to stand. True, the Hebrew passage is probably 1,500 years later than the Egyptian, though it may already have been old when it became embedded in the Second Book of Samuel, some time after 1000 B. C. But the distinction is not wholly one of date, for even in later times the Egyptians never produced anything quite equal to this for

---

[1] A place in the Delta marshes whither Isis withdrew with her young son Horus to protect him from his uncle Set.

magnificence and power of description. The ship of their genius swam in calmer waters.

Of the secular poetry of this early period in Egypt nothing has survived except a song of victory from the tomb of a noble of the VIth Dynasty who had led a successful expedition to Syria.[1]

This army returned in safety,
Having hacked up the land of the Sand-dwellers.
This army returned in safety,
Having trodden down the land of the Sand-dwellers.
This army returned in safety,
Having destroyed its fortresses.
This army returned in safety,
Having cut down its figs and its vines.
This army returned in safety,
Having consumed all its [troops].
This army returned in safety,
Having slain troops therein, in many tens-of-thousands.
This army returned in safety,
[Having brought] thence very many [troops] as living prisoners.

It is unfortunately not possible to trace the development of Egyptian lyric poetry from this early period into the New Empire, for examples are lacking from the Middle Kingdom. There is, however, one exception, a collection of hymns to King Senusret III,[2] who ruled from 1887 to 1849 B. C. Of the four hymns which are almost completely preserved three show the simple device of beginning each line with the same phrase. Whether the separate lines have a fixed metrical structure we cannot of course say; they are, however, all of approximately the same length, and the

---

[1] Sethe, *Urkunden des Alten Reichs*, pp. 103–4. Tomb of Una.

[2] From a papyrus found at El-Lâhûn (often called Kahun in Egyptological literature). See F. Ll. Griffith, *Hieratic Papyri from Kahun and Gurob* (London, 1898), Plates I–III.

existence of metre is probable. I give here a translation of
the first four hymns.

Hail to thee, Khakaure, our Horus Divine-of-Existence!
Who protects the land, and widens its boundaries,
Who holds the foreign lands in check with his crown.
Who embraces the Two Lands [1] within the compass of his arms,
  Who [seizes] the nations in his grasp.
Who slays the Bowmen [2] without stroke of the club,
  Who shoots the arrow without drawing the bow-string.
Fear of him hath smitten the Anu [3] in their land;
  Dread of him hath slain the Nine Bows.[4]
His knife hath caused to die thousands of the Bowmen
  [Ere yet they could] set foot on his frontier.
Who shoots the arrow even as does Sekhmet,[5]
  When he overthrows thousands of them that know not his might.
The tongue of his majesty controls Nubia,
  His words put to flight the Asiatics.
Sole One of youthful vigour, who fights for his frontier,
  Who suffers not his subjects to grow weary,
But causes the folk to sleep through till dawn.
His young warriors sleep,
  For his heart is their protection.
His decrees have created his boundaries,
  His word hath drawn together the Two Lands.

How joyful are [the gods]; thou hast established their offerings.
How joyful are thy [lands]; thou hast fixed their boundaries.
How joyful are thy ancestors; thou hast increased their portion.
How joyful is Egypt in thy might; thou hast protected the old order.
How joyful are the people in thy government; thy mighty power hath
  suppressed usurpation.[6]

  [1] Egypt, Upper and Lower.
  [2] Perhaps specifically Asiatics at this period.
  [3] Probably Nubians.
  [4] An early term for Egypt's enemies in general.
  [5] The lion-headed goddess of destruction.
  [6] In contrast to 'the old order'.

How joyful are the Two Lands in thy dread renown; thou hast widened their possessions.

How joyful are thy young conscripts; thou hast made them to flourish.

How joyful are thy aged ones; thou hast given them youth.

How joyful are the Two Lands in thy might; thou hast protected their walls.

How great is the lord of his city; he is the equivalent of a million, thousands of others are but as a few.

How great is the lord of his city; he is a dyke damming the stream to prevent floods.

How great is the lord of his city; he is a cool chamber, suffering all men to sleep through till dawn.

How great is the lord of his city; he is a stronghold with walls of copper of Shesem.[1]

How great is the lord of his city; he is a refuge whose hand does not tremble.

How great is the lord of his city; he is a sanctuary that saves the fearful one from his enemy.

How great is the lord of his city; he is a cool and refreshing shade in summer.

How great is the lord of his city; he is a corner warm and dry in wintertime.

How great is the lord of his city; he is a hill that wards off the blast when heaven rages.

How great is the lord of his city; he is like Sekhmet[2] *to foes who set foot upon his boundary.*

He hath come to us that he may seize the Land of Upper Egypt; the Double Crown is placed upon his head.

He hath come to us, he hath united the Two Lands, he hath joined the reed [3] *to the bee.*[3]

He hath come to us, he hath ruled the people of Egypt, he hath taken the desert into his possession.

He hath come to us, he hath protected the Two Lands, he hath appeased the Two Lands.

[1] Perhaps Sinai.   [2] See p. 67, note 5.
[3] The emblems of Upper and Lower Egypt respectively.

He hath come to us, he hath made the people of Egypt to live, he hath destroyed its afflictions.

He hath come to us, he hath made the populace to live, he hath opened the throats of the people.[1]

He hath come to us, he hath trampled upon the foreign countries, he hath smitten the Anu who knew not the fear of him.

He hath come to us, he hath [protected] his boundary, he hath rescued him who was robbed.

He hath come to us, . . . honoured old age, by reason of what his might hath brought to us.

He hath come, [he hath enabled us to rear] our children and bury our aged . . . .

This group of hymns marks a definite advance on anything which has come down to us from the Old Kingdom. It is not without a certain noble simplicity, and the imagery of the third hymn shows how firmly metaphor was now established in the Egyptian mind as a quality of lyric writing. It contains numbers of phrases and ideas which can be paralleled in Hebrew song, more particularly in the Psalms. With these, however, it can hardly be compared in literary merit; it is too stiff and monotonous, it lacks their freedom and variety. It compares unfavourably even with some of the earlier efforts of Hebrew poetry, such as the Song of Deborah and the Lament of David for Saul and Jonathan. At the same time it is very much older than these. From the Egyptian point of view it is important as almost the sole example of Middle Kingdom poetry which has survived.

When we pass to the New Empire we are at once confronted by a wealth of lyric writing, much of which is clearly of contemporary date, while some is equally clearly based on older originals. It is, however, quite impossible to disentangle the older and the newer elements, and we can only take the material as it is and regard it as representative of the lyric poetry of the New Empire. It consists to a large extent of hymns to the gods, and songs of praise and victory

[1] So enabling them to breathe more easily.

addressed to the kings. It will be convenient to begin with the latter; the examples chosen are designed partly to show Egyptian lyric poetry at its best, partly to display its variety and so to facilitate a comparison with that of the Hebrews.

We may fitly begin with a victory poem of King Tuthmosis III, the founder of the Egyptian empire in Syria.[1] It is inscribed upon a fine stela which was set up in the temple of Amun at Karnak, and consists of a laudatory address by the god himself to his son the king, who is regarded as entering the temple in triumph after a successful campaign. Some of it appears to be in prose, but there is a central section which is clearly metrical, and this I quote in full. The structure of the stanzas is too obvious to need comment.

I have come [2]
That I may cause thee to tread down the great ones of Phoenicia,
That I may strew them beneath thy feet throughout their lands;
That I may cause them to behold thy majesty as Lord of Brilliance
When thou shinest in their faces as my image.

I have come
That I may cause thee to tread down them that are in Asia,
And smite the heads of the Aamu [3] of Retenu;
That I may cause them to behold thy majesty equipped with thy panoply,
When thou takest up the weapons of war in the chariot.

I have come
That I may cause thee to tread down the eastern land,
And trample upon them that are in the regions of God's Land; [4]
That I may cause them to behold thy majesty like Seshed,[5]
Who scatters his flame in fire when he sends forth his effluence.

---

[1] Sethe, *Urkunden der 18. Dynastie,* in Steindorff, *Urk. des ägyptischen Altertums,* IV. Abteilung, pp. 610 ff. (Leipzig, 1905 ff.).

[2] The speaker is the god Amen-Re.   [3] Syrians.

[4] A term used of various countries east of Egypt: Punt, Arabia and even Syria.   [5] A baneful constellation.

I have come
That I may cause thee to tread down the western land,
  Keftiu [1] *and Asy* [2] *are beneath thy might;*
That I may cause them to behold thy majesty as a young bull,
  Stout of heart, sharp of horn, who may not be attacked.

I have come
That I may cause thee to tread down them that are in their marshes(?),
  While the lands of Methen tremble beneath the fear of thee;
That I may cause them to behold thy majesty as a crocodile,
  Lord of Fear in the water, unapproachable.

I have come
That I may cause thee to tread down them that are in the islands
  That are in the midst of the Ocean beneath thy war-cry;
That I may cause them to behold thy majesty as an avenger [3]
  Appearing triumphant upon the back of his victim.

I have come
That I may cause thee to tread down Libya
  And Iuthentiu through the power of thy might;
That I may cause them to behold thy majesty as a fierce lion
  When thou makest them heaps of corpses in their valleys.

I have come
That I may cause thee to tread down the uttermost parts of the lands,
  While all that the Ocean encircles is seized in thy grasp;
That I may cause them to behold thy majesty as Lord of the Wing, [4]
  Who seizes upon that which he beholds even as he desires.

I have come
That I may cause thee to tread down them who are in the Front of
  Earth,
  And bind the Sand-dwellers as prisoners.
That I may cause them to behold thy majesty as a jackal of Upper
  Egypt,
  Lord of Speeding, a runner who traverses the Two Lands.

---

[1] Either Crete or part of Cilicia.   [2] A coast-land in North Syria.
[3] A frequent epithet of Horus, who avenges his father Osiris on his
uncle Set ('his victim').   [4] Epithet of Horus.

I have come
That I may cause thee to tread down the Anu of Nubia,
  And as far as Shat [1] *is in thy grip;*
That I may cause them to behold thy majesty like thy Two Brothers
  Whose hands I have joined for thee in victory.

This hymn is too formal and too lacking in variety to be fine literature. A much better poem of a freer and more imaginative type is the Hymn to Ramesses II which has survived on several stelae in and near the great rock-temple built by the king at Abu Simbel in Nubia.[2] The inscription begins with the king's titulary, supplemented by a number of laudatory epithets. Then follows the poem itself, each stanza ending with the words ' King of Upper and Lower Egypt Ramesses '. The following quotations will give an idea of the quality of the writing:

Who treadeth down the land of the Hittites and maketh it a heap of corpses, like Sekhmet when she rages after a pestilence. Who sendeth forth his arrows against them and hath the mastery over their bodies. The princes of every foreign land have come forth from their country wakeful and without sleep, their bodies faint. Their gifts are an assortment of the products of their land. Their armed men and their children are in the forefront thereof in order to beg for peace from his majesty, King of Upper and Lower Egypt Ramesses.

Their princes are afraid when they behold him, for he is like Month in might and strength, as he cuts off their heads like the son of Nut. He is as a bull with sharp horns, mighty in seizing(?), releasing only when he hath made an end of his foes. King of Upper and Lower Egypt Ramesses.

Strong lion, driving out . . . by reason of his loud roar, uttering his voice in the valley of the wild game. King of Upper and Lower Egypt Ramesses.

Jackal swift of stride in seeking out him that hath attacked him, traversing the circuit of earth in a moment of time.

---

[1] A country in the far south.
[2] Lepsius, *Denkmaeler aus Aegypten und Aethiopien*, iii, 195 a.

Divine and noble hawk, equipped with wings(?), swooping down upon the small and the great, that he may cause them to know themselves no more. King of Upper and Lower Egypt Ramesses.

Who putteth to flight the Asiatics, fighting upon the battlefield. They break their bows asunder and are given over to the fire. His might hath the mastery over them, as it were a flame when it hath seized upon the stubble(?), and a storm-wind is behind it; like fierce fire when it hath tasted of the raging flame, and every one that is in it becometh ashes. King of Upper and Lower Egypt Ramesses.

Ruler mighty in slaying them that know not his name; like unto a tempest that howleth loudly upon the sea, and its waves are like mountains and none can approach it, but every one that is in it is sunk in the Underworld. King of Upper and Lower Egypt Ramesses.

King that shineth forth in the White Crown, strength of Egypt, wise in warfare on the field of battle, valiant in the mellay; furious warrior, stout of heart, who setteth his arms as it were a wall about his soldiers. King of Upper and Lower Egypt Ramesses.

This is fine poetry. It marks an advance on the victory poem of Tuthmosis in every way. Its images, above all, are bolder, and they are not limited to mere epithets of the king but are worked out in some detail. In this respect the work comes much nearer to some of the Hebrew Psalms than to earlier Egyptian hymns of this type, and, could it have been done into English by one of the translators of the version of 1611, and inserted with due change of proper names in the Book of Psalms, I question whether it would ever have been detected as an intrusion. If it had been, it would not have been through the inferiority of the author's power of imagination.

This hymn, however, is not by any means the only example of its kind in the New Empire, and I have the less hesitation in quoting another because, while admitting the high merit of the Hebrews in the domain of lyric poetry, and the superiority of what they have handed down to us to what has come to us from Egypt and Babylonia, I am anxious to

do the Egyptians every justice by showing that in the quality
of its work the Ramesses hymn does not stand alone.

The Hymn of Victory of Merenptah is inscribed on a
stela of black granite set up in his mortuary temple in
Thebes, mainly in commemoration of a victory which saved
Egypt from a serious threat from Libya.[1] This monument
is commonly known as the Israel-stela, for among the names
of the conquered peoples occurs that of Israel. The usual
heading, date and titles are followed by a passage which is
doubtless poetical in form as well as in substance:

> *The telling of his victories in all lands; making every land to
> know, that the beauty of his valiant deeds may be seen;*
>
> *Even King of Upper and Lower Egypt Merenptah, the Bull,
> lord of might, who slays his enemies, beauteous upon the field of
> valour when he thrusts.*
>
> *A sun has come into being, dispersing the rain-cloud that was
> over Egypt, causing Timuris [2] to see the rays of the sun.*
>
> *Removing the mountain of copper from the neck of the folk,
> that he might give breath to the people who were confined.*
>
> *Making Memphis [3] to rejoice over her foes, and Ptah [4] to exult
> over his enemies.*
>
> *Opening the gates of the stronghold that were closed and causing
> its temples to receive their offering-meals;*
>
> *Even King of Upper and Lower Egypt Merenptah, strengthen-
> ing alone the hearts of hundreds of thousands; at the sight of whom
> the breath of life enters into men's nostrils.*
>
> *In whose lifetime the land of Temeh [5] is broken, and eternal
> fear placed in the hearts of the Meshwesh.[6]*
>
> *He put to flight the Libyans who had set foot in Egypt, a great
> fear is in their hearts by reason of Timuris.*
>
> *Their advancing troops have turned their backs, their feet stand
> not firm but seek flight.*

[1] Petrie, *Six Temples at Thebes* (Quaritch), Pl. XIV. First translated
by Spiegelberg in *Zeitschr. für äg. Sprache*, xxxiv, pp. 1 ff.

[2] A name for Egypt.

[3] Memphis was directly threatened by the Libyan invasion of the
Delta.   [4] God of Memphis.   [5] Libya.   [6] A Libyan tribe.

Their bowmen cast away their bows; the heart of their swift ones is wretched with marching.

They loosen their water-skins and throw them on the ground; their knapsacks are torn off and cast away.

The wretched enemy chief of Libya fled in the depth of night, alone, with no plume upon his head; his feet were weary.

His wives were captured before his face; the food of his table was carried away, and he had no water in his water-skin to keep him alive.

The faces of his brethren were fierce to slay him; one fought with another among his captains.

Their tents were burnt and made into ashes; all his goods were as food for the soldiery.

Later there follows an admirable passage describing the joy caused in Egypt by the victory:

Great rejoicing hath arisen in Egypt, and jubilation is gone forth from the towns of Timuris.

Men tell of the victories that Merenptah hath won in the land of the Tehenu.[1]

How men love him, the victorious ruler; how they magnify the King among the gods; how fortunate is he, lord of command!

How pleasant it is to sit chatting![2] Men go freely upon the road and there is no fear in men's hearts.

Strongholds are left to themselves; the wells are open and accessible(?) to messengers.

The battlements of the walls are restful, and it is the sun[3] that shall awaken their watchmen.

The Mazoi[4] are sleeping, and the Nau[5] and Tekten[5] wander about the tillage as they list.

[1] Yet another name for the Libyans.

[2] I translate so in spite of Gardiner's criticism of this rendering in *Proceedings of the Soc. of Biblical Archaeology*, 1915, 12 May, pp. 121–2. Both his grammatical objections seem to be nullified by ll. 24–5 of the stela itself, and I do not in any case understand what his rendering means.   [3] And not, as recently, a Libyan alarm.

[4] Nubian mercenaries in the Egyptian army.

[5] Mercenaries from the oases.

The herds of the pasture are left to roam; the herdsmen cross not the waters of the stream.[1]

There is no crying aloud in the night of men calling Stop! and Come hither! in a strange tongue.

Men come and go singing, and there is no cry of men mourning.

Towns are re-peopled anew, and he that hath sown his corn shall also eat it.

Re hath turned him again unto Egypt.

As a last example of this kind of lyric I give some quotations from a song of praise to King Ramesses IV. It was written on a flake of limestone by a scribe of the Theban Necropolis called Amennekht, who is known to us from other sources. Maspero's copy, published fifty years ago,[2] is very faulty (he notes that the original is both faded and damaged), and a complete or certain translation is impossible. The copy is dated in Year 4 of the king's reign. The composition is clearly a song of congratulation to the king on the return of peace and settled government after a period of internal disturbance.

O happy day! Heaven and earth rejoice, for thou art the great lord of Egypt.

They that had fled have come again to their towns, and they that were hidden have come forth again.

They that hungered are satisfied and happy, they that thirsted are drunken.

They that were naked are clad in fine linen, and they that were tattered (?) have fine garments.

They that were in prison are set free, and he that was . . . is filled with joy.

They that were in uproar in this land are at peace. High Niles

---

[1] These words, if correct, must mean that the cattle can be trusted to wander even on the Libyan side of the stream. The locality in the poet's mind is the West Delta.

[2] *Recueil de travaux*, ii, pp. 116–7. See too Spiegelberg in *Orientalistische Literaturzeitung*, xxx, cols. 73 ff.

*have come forth from their caverns to make glad the hearts of the
people.*

*As for the widows, their houses stand open, and they suffer
travellers to enter.*

Maidens rejoice and sing their songs of gladness.

*Ships rejoice on the deep, for the sea is waveless (?); they come to
land with wind and oars.*

*They are filled with joy when we say 'King Hekmare chosen of
Amun weareth the White Crown,*

The son of Re, Ramesses, hath assumed the office of his father.'

In the domain of religious literature three hymns stand
out for special notice, the Hymn to the Nile, Akhenaten's
Hymn to the Sun's Disk, and the Great Hymn to Amun.
The first begins:[1]

*Praise to thee, O Nile, that issuest forth from the earth and comest to
nourish the dwellers in Egypt. Secret of movement, a darkness in
the daytime . . .*

*That waterest the meadows which Re hath created to nourish all
cattle.*

*That givest drink to the desert places which are far from water; his
dew it is that falleth from heaven.*

*Beloved of the Earth-God, controller of the Corn-God, that maketh
every workshop of Ptah to flourish.*

*Lord of fish, that maketh the water-fowl to go up stream, without
a bird falling . . .*

*That maketh barley and createth wheat, that maketh the temples to
keep festival.*

*If he is sluggish the nostrils are stopped up, and all men are brought
low;*

---

[1] Very corrupt school copies are preserved in Pap. Anastasi VII,
7.7 ff. and Pap. Sallier II, 11.6 ff. There are also fragments in a Turin
papyrus (unpublished) and three ostraca. The Golenishchef Ostracon
serves partly to reveal the almost incredible corruption of the Anastasi
and Sallier copies, partly to make possible a continuous though very
tentative translation of the first part of the hymn. Beyond its limits
translation is almost hopeless.

The offerings of the gods are diminished, and millions perish from among mankind;

The greedy man causes confusion throughout the land, and great and small are brought to naught.

Men are changed when he attacks; Khnum hath fashioned him.[1]

When he arises earth rejoices and all men are glad; every jaw laughs and every tooth is uncovered.

Bringer of nourishment, plenteous of sustenance, creating all things good.

Lord of reverence, sweet of savour, appeasing evil.

Creating herbage for the cattle, causing sacrifice to be made to every god.

He is in the Underworld, in heaven and upon earth . . .

Filling the barns and widening the granaries; giving to the poor.

Causing trees to grow according to the uttermost desire, so that men go not in lack of them.

Akhenaten's Hymn to the Disk (about 1370 B.C.) deserves much of the praise which has been lavished upon it. The parallels with the 104th Psalm may be quite fortuitous, but there are several circumstances which tend to make it a document of importance in the literary history of the world. In the first place it is the earliest truly monotheistic hymn which the world has produced. In the second place the desire of the king to break with tradition fortunately closed to him that morass of mythology from which most earlier hymns had drawn their material. And in the third place it breathes that delight in nature and her works which the religion of the Disk seems to have brought so much into prominence. In view of its importance it is quoted here in full.[2]

Adoration of the Disk by King Akhenaten and Queen Nefertete.

Thou shinest beautiful on the horizon of heaven, O Living Disk who didst live from the beginning. When thou risest in the eastern

---

[1] This line is clearly corrupt.

[2] For the text see N. de G. Davies, *The Rock Tombs of El Amarna* (Egypt Exploration Fund, London, 1908), vi, Pl. XXVII.

horizon thou fillest every land with thy beauty. When thou art beautiful, great, brilliant, high over every land, thy rays embrace the lands even to the limit of that which thou hast created. Thou art Re. Thou bringest them all (the lands) that thou mayest bind them for thy beloved son. Even though thou art afar thy beams are upon the earth; thou art in their faces . . . thy goings. When thou settest in the western horizon the earth is in darkness after the fashion of death. They (men) sleep in their bed-chambers covered up; the eye beholdeth not its fellow. Men may steal away their goods though they be beneath their heads, and they know it not. Every lion cometh forth from his den, and every snake biteth. Darkness is . . . and the earth is in silence, he who made them having gone to rest in his horizon.

When thou risest in the morning and shinest as Aten by day thou dost put to flight the darkness and givest (forth) thy rays. The Two Lands[1] rejoice, they awake and stand on their feet, for thou hast aroused them. They wash their limbs and take up their clothes, their arms do adoration to thy rising. All the land performs its labours. All cattle rejoice in their pastures. The trees and herbs grow green. Birds and winged things (come forth) from their nests, their wings doing adoration to thy spirit. All goats skip on their feet, all that flies takes wing; they begin to live when thou risest on them. Ships ply upstream and downstream likewise; every path is opened by reason of thy rising. The fish in the stream leap before thy face, thy beams are in the depths of the ocean.

Creator of issue in women, maker of seed in mankind, who quickenest the son in the womb of his mother, soothing him that he may not weep, nurse within the womb, who givest breath to quicken all whom he would create. When he comes forth from the womb (to the . . .) on the day of his birth thou dost open his mouth . . . and dost provide for his needs. When the chick in the egg cries within the shell thou givest him breath within it to quicken him; thou hast made for him his strength (?) to break it from within the egg. When he comes forth from the egg to chirp with all his might (?) he goes upon his two legs when he comes forth from it.

How manifold are thy works! They are concealed from (us).

[1] Upper and Lower Egypt.

O sole god to whom no other is like! Thou didst create the earth according to thy desire when thou wast alone, men and cattle, all goats, and all that is upon the earth and goeth upon its feet, and all that is in the sky and flieth with its wings. The foreign lands too, Syria and Ethiopia, and the land of Egypt. Thou puttest each man in his place, thou providest for his needs, each one having his sustenance and his days reckoned.

Their tongues are distinguished in speech; their characters likewise and their complexions are different. Thou hast distinguished the nations.

Thou createst the Nile in the Underworld and bringest it forth according to thy will to give life to mankind, even as thou didst create them for thyself, lord of all of them, who art weary by reason of them, lord of every land, who risest for them, Disk of the day, great of might.

All the far countries, thou makest them to live. Thou hast set a Nile in the heaven, that he may come down for them and make streams upon the hills like the ocean, to water their fields beside their villages. How perfect are thy counsels, thou lord of eternity! The Nile in heaven [1] *is for the foreign lands and the wild animals of every foreign land that run upon their feet, but the Nile when he comes forth from the Underworld is for Egypt. Thy rays nurse all fields; when thou shinest they live and grow for thee. Thou createst the seasons in order to nourish all that thou hast created, the winter to cool them, the summer heat . . . .*

Thou hast made a heaven afar to shine in it and to see all that thou hast made. Thou art alone, thou shinest in thy form as the Living Disk, whether thou risest or shinest, or art afar off or drawest near. Thou didst create millions of existences out of thyself alone, cities, towns, lands, paths, and streams. Every eye beholds thee over against it when thou art the Disk of the day above . . . in order that thou mightest not see . . . which thou hast made.

Thou art in my heart. There is none other that knoweth thee save thy son Akhenaten. Thou didst grant him to understand thy counsels and thy might when the earth came into being in thy hand, even as thou didst make them. [2] *When thou risest they live, when thou settest*

---

[1] *I.e.*, rain.   [2] Mankind, to judge by what follows.

they die. Thou art length of days in thyself. In thee men live. Eyes are on thy beauty until thou settest. All labour is set aside when thou settest in the west: but when ⟨thou⟩ risest [work] for the king is made to proceed apace. All men that run upon their feet since thou didst found the earth thou hast raised them up for thy son who came forth from thyself, even Akhenaten.

This represents a great advance on any hymn which can be quoted from the Old Kingdom. Expression is freer, and the poet's originality is so much greater that he can afford to spurn the simple devices of earlier days, such as the cruder forms of parallelism.

The great Cairo Hymn to Amun is not entirely free from the defects of earlier Egyptian hymns, notably the tiresome repetition of the epithets of the gods and the endless mythological allusions, many of which are meaningless to us. At the same time, though it falls behind Akhenaten's hymn to the Disk in poetic qualities, yet it is historically important, for it shows that this last was not the mushroom growth that some would have us believe it was, but was based to a great extent on older material. The following will give an idea of the Cairo hymn:

Praise of Re in Karnak, shining in might in the House of the Obelisk;
God of Heliopolis, Lord of the Festival of the New Moon,
For whom are performed the festivals of the sixth day and of the last quarter,
Sovereign and Lord of all the gods,
Falcon (?)[1] that dwelleth in the Horizon,
Chief of mankind and of the Underworld,
Whose name is hidden from his children in this his name of Amun.[2]
Hail to thee, that sittest in peace ⟨in thy bark⟩,
Lord of joy, shining in might!
Lord of the crown, with lofty feathers,
With beautiful diadem, and tall white crown.

[1] Corrupt.   [2] *I.e.*, 'The Hidden One.'

The gods love to behold thee when the Double Crown rests upon thy forehead.

The love of thee is spread abroad through the Two Lands.

Thy rays shine in men's eyes.

It is well with mankind when thou risest, albeit the cattle are weary (sic) when thou shinest.

Thy love is in the southern heaven, and thy sweetness in the northern heaven.

Thy beauty carries away hearts, love of thee makes faint the arms;

Thy lovely form makes the hands weak and the heart fail for looking upon thee.

Thou art the One who madest all that which exists,

The One Alone who didst create that which is.

From whose eyes came forth mankind and in whose mouth the gods came into being.

Who madest pasture for all manner of cattle and the fruit trees for man.

Who didst bring forth that on which the fish in the stream might live and the birds that fly in the heaven.

Who gavest breath to that which is within the egg and didst endow the young of the snake with life.

Who madest that on which the birds might live, and the worms, yea and flying things likewise.

Who didst provide for the needs of the mice in their holes and gavest life to the birds in every tree.

Hail to thee who didst bring forth all these things, Sole One, many-handed!

Who spendest the night long awake while all men sleep, seeking the comfort of his (sic) cattle.

Amun ⟨in⟩ whom all things abide, Atum, Horus of the Two Horizons,

Praise to thee, say they all, praise to thee that thou concernest thyself with us!

Obeisance to thee for that thou hast created us!

Hail to thee! say all cattle. Praise to thee! says every foreign land, as high as is the heaven, as wide as is the earth, as deep as is the ocean.

The gods do obeisance before thy majesty, exalting the might of him
   that created them, rejoicing at the approach of him that begat them.
   They say unto thee:
Welcome in peace, father of the fathers of all gods, who hast hung
   the heaven and fixed (?) the earth,
Who madest that which exists and didst create that which is.
Sovereign, chief of the gods! We revere thy might even as thou didst
   create us,
We make ⟨rejoicing⟩ to thee for that thou didst make us,
We give thee praise for that thou concernest thyself with us.

The Hebrew counterpart of these psalms is to be found in
the hymns to the deity scattered over several books of the
Old Testament, but mainly collected in the Book of the
Psalms of David so-called. Of these I need say very little,
for their outstanding merit is obvious.[1] No doubt there are
passages in the Egyptian hymns above quoted, and in
others, which will stand comparison with anything in the
Hebrew, but when we add together all that Egypt has left
us in this kind of writing there is but little to set against the
Book of Psalms alone. In no department of literature do the
Hebrews more completely outdistance their masters[2] and
their competitors than in this. The world has produced no
more spontaneous outburst. Think of its immense quantity
—and what we have is doubtless but a selection of what
existed—and of the bewildering variety of thoughts and
images with which it is filled. How neatly, in many of the
songs, the mood or thought is indicated in the opening verse,
and how admirably and succinctly worked out in what
follows! How beautifully each psalm is rounded off, neither
too short nor too long, complete in itself, like an Étude of
Chopin! And lastly, how brightly they shine, especially as

[1] My readers will doubtless get the same pleasure as I did from
reading, on this point, the collection of essays edited by D. C. Simpson
under the title *The Psalmists*, Oxford, 1926.

[2] That the Hebrews owed something to both Babylonian and Egyptian psalmody is now generally recognized, though the amount of the
debt is a matter of dispute: see *op. cit.*, pp. 15 ff., 109 ff., 177 ff.

against the Egyptian, by reason of their higher ethical tone, that consciousness of moral responsibility, of sin and forgiveness, whose total absence is such a remarkable feature of the Egyptian hymns!

Here we may conveniently turn for a moment to consider what Babylonia has to show in the department of lyric poetry. The lyric muse, like the epic, was there entirely devoted to the service of religion. 'The lyric pieces of the cuneiform literature' writes Weber[1] 'are wholly religious in character. Profane songs, folk-songs of general content, drinking-songs, love-songs, such as occur, for example, in Egyptian literature, are up to the present unknown to us from a single example. That the Babylonians too loved and drank and sang of love and wine like all men may be taken for granted; it is proved indeed beyond all doubt by representations in their reliefs. Yet the fact remains that the productions of the gayer muse have not yet come to light among the treasures of the cuneiform literature available to us.'

These religious lyrics may be divided into three types, prayers, hymns and psalms, which, however, are very apt to overrun one another's boundaries. Like almost all Babylonian literary productions they have been taken up into the liturgical collections of the temples, with the result that all chronological and personal application has gone from them. In diction the best of them show (I again quote Weber[2]) 'a remarkable vigour of thought, a boldness and clearness of imagery, and a disproportionately great wealth of expressions for general conceptions and individual feelings. It must, however, be admitted that the number of texts which stand out by reason of these qualities is comparatively very small, though it may at any moment be increased in a surprising manner by new finds. Among the texts at present available those of average merit are very definitely the more numerous, those which show a "typical and conventional character and few individual traits". . . . . In the

[1] *Lit.*, p. 115.   [2] *Lit.*, pp. 121–2.

main the typical use of images and expressions is naturally closely connected with the subject of the poem. In the hymns it is the qualities of the god to be revered, in the psalms and prayers the underlying mood, which in general cause similar forms of expression to keep recurring within the particular kind of poetry; these often become mere formulas which keep repeating themselves word for word.'

The following quotations from the great hymn to Shamash the sun-god[1] will illustrate at its best the Babylonian genius for hymn-writing:

The mighty hills are surrounded by thy glory;
The flat lands are filled with thy brightness.
Thou hast power over the mountains, and lookest over the earth;
Thou dost hang up the hems of the land, in the innermost part of
heaven.
The men of the lands, thou watchest over them all;
Thou dost watch over all that King Ea the Adviser hath created.
Thou givest pasture to all living creatures,
Yea! thou art the shepherd of all that is above and beneath.
Thou travellest constantly in the heaven,
Thou comest day by day to lighten the earth.
Thou dost watch over the Underworld of Ea, of Azagsud and the
Anunnaki;[2]
Thou rulest the whole Upperworld of inhabited places.
Shepherd of what is beneath, guardian of what is above;
Controller of light for the universe, Thou, O Shamash!
Thou stridest over the sea, the broad, the distant,
Whose innermost depths even the Igigi[3] know not.
O Shamash! Thy beams penetrate the deep waters;
The bottoms of the sea behold thy light.

[1] Known to Assyriologists as K 3182. It consists of four columns containing about 420 lines, and is preserved only in Semitic. Unfortunately not one of the four columns is completely preserved. I have used the translations of H. Zimmern (*Der alte Orient*, xiii, pp. 22 ff.) and Jastrow (*Die Religion Babyloniens und Assyriens*, i. 432 ff.), not without being disconcerted by their frequent divergence.

[2] Earthly spirits.   [3] Heavenly spirits.

Among all the Igigi is none that travaileth like thee;
  Among the gods of the whole universe is none that surpasseth thee.
At thy rising the gods of the land assemble;
  Thy awful brightness overpowereth the earth.
Men's designs in the speech of all lands
  Thou knowest, and observest their goings.
The whole of mankind looketh up to thee,
  O Shamash! The universe longeth for thy light.

Thou destroyest the horn of him who deviseth evil;
  Thou overturnest the place of him who planneth oppression.
Thou causest the unjust judge to see confinement,
  And punishest the corrupt and the evil leader.
But he that is incorruptible and maketh intercession for the weak
  Is well pleasing to Shamash, and his days are lengthened.
The conscientious judge that giveth just judgement
  Prepareth for himself a palace; his habitation is a dwelling of
    princes.
He that lendeth at high interest, what shall it profit him?
  He defraudeth himself of gain; he emptieth his purse.
He that lendeth at low interest, and receiveth a skekel for . . . ;
  It is well pleasing to Shamash, and prolongeth life.

He that oppresseth the dependant is marked down with the pen;
  They that do evil, their seed shall not abide.
They whose mouth is full of lies, thus dost thou unto them,
  Thou burnest and dissolvest the words of their mouth.
Thou hearest the oppressed as thou passest over them and searchest
  out their rights;
  Each and all are in thy hand.
Thou guidest their oracles, thou freest what was bound.
  Thou hearkenest, O Shamash! to prayer, to entreaty and praise,
Prostration, kneeling, whispered prayer and bowings-down.
  From the depths of his throat the wretched crieth to thee;
The failing, the feeble, the tormented, the poor,
  Cometh ever to thee with song of woe or petition:
He whose family is afar, whose town is distant.
  The shepherd cometh to thee with the produce of the field;

He that . . . in rebellion, the shepherd oppressed by the foe,
  O Shamash! cometh to thee, for he treadeth a path of terror.
The travelling merchant, the trader bearing his purse
  . . . cometh to thee, the fisher of the deep.
The hunter, the slaughterer, the custodian of cattle,
  In the . . . ; the bird-catcher cometh to thee.
The robber, the thief, even though foes of Shamash;
  From the desert track the wanderer cometh to thee.
The wandering dead, the fleeting shades,
  O Shamash! come to thee . . .

  At the time of prayer thou shoutest aloud for joy and gladness,
Thou eatest, thou drinkest their unmixed wine, and fine beer from
    the cask.
  When they offer thee beer, even fine beer, thou acceptest it.

  The wishes that they cherished thou sufferest them to accomplish;
Them that kneel to thee thou absolvest and makest clean:
  Thou acceptest the praise of them that praise thee.
But they fear thee and revere thy name,
  Men bow them down ever before thy greatness.
Them that are foolish of tongue and speak that which is ungodly,
  That which hath neither front nor back, like clouds
That pass over the face of the wide earth
  And rest upon the high mountains,
The god Lakhmu shall overwhelm them, even the lord of terror.
  The harvest of the sea, all that cometh out of the deep,
The tribute which the stream payeth, O Shamash! lieth before thee.
  What mountains are not covered with thy gleam?
What places are not warmed by the beams of thy light?
  Thou who lightenest the darkness and brightenest the gloom,
Who puttest to flight the darkness and givest light to the wide earth,
  Who brightenest the day and sendest down the midday heat upon
    earth.

Even these scattered examples suffice to show that this
hymn to the sun-god is a very noble piece of poetry, and it is
a tragedy that the damaged state of the tablets which con-

tain it prevents a more complete and certain translation. Even as it stands, however, it proves that, at any rate occasionally, the Babylonian reached a standard of lyric composition which is at least as high as anything yet known to us from the Egyptian hymns and comes very close to the best work of the Book of Psalms. This hymn is longer, and perhaps contains more variety of thought, image and expression, than any of the Egyptian hymns. It differs from them, too, in laying much more stress on the moral aspect of man's relation to the god.

Space forbids that I should give further examples of this type of literature from Babylonia, though that given does not by any means stand alone.[1] It would not be difficult, in fact, to make a collection of such hymns which would in quantity far surpass what we have from Egypt and be almost comparable in bulk with the Book of Psalms. As literature it would be inferior to these last, for it would, as a whole, lack their variety and vigour of expression, and would often annoy by its vain repetitions; altogether it would stand on a somewhat lower plane of thought and morality. With some such body of hymns as this the Hebrews must have come into contact during the exile, and probably before it. We may perhaps never learn the nature and extent of the debt which they owed to it, nor the date at which that debt was contracted. We can, however, assert with confidence that they borrowed nothing which they did not improve upon.

It is impossible to leave the question of religious poetry without a reference to a curious little group of documents which have been recovered from the tombstones of humble persons who lived in Thebes under the XIXth Dynasty. From the religious point of view they sound a note of personal humility which we hear in Egypt at no other period.[2] As

---

[1] For other examples see Zimmern, *Babylonische Hymnen und Gebete*, in *Der alte Orient*, vii, pp. 3 ff. and xiii, pp. 3 ff.

[2] Gunn in *Journ. Eg. Arch.*, iii, pp. 81 ff., and references there quoted.

literature, too, they are valuable, for they give us a curiously close parallel to the penitential psalms of both Palestine and Babylonia. Here is an excerpt from a stela set up by a man who had been struck blind as a punishment for swearing falsely by the god Ptah: [1]

I am a man who swore falsely by Ptah, Lord of Truth;
And he caused me to behold darkness by day.
I will declare his might to him that knows him not and to him that
  knows him,
To small and great.
Be ye ware of Ptah, Lord of Truth.
Lo, he will not overlook the deed of any man.
Refrain ye from uttering the name of Ptah falsely;
Lo, he that uttereth it falsely,
Lo, he falleth.
He caused me to be as the dogs of the street,
I being in his hand:
He caused men and gods to mark me,
I being as a man that has wrought abomination against his
  Lord.
Righteous was Ptah, Lord of Truth, toward me,
When he chastised me.
Be merciful to me; look upon me, that thou mayest be merciful. [2]

Here is another, from a stela dedicated to Amun by a certain draughtsman Nebre and his son Khay, in thanks for the recovery from an illness of another son of Nebre, Nekhtamun. [3]

Praise-giving to Amun:
  I will make him adoration in his name,
  I will give him praise as far as the height of heaven
  And as far as the breadth of earth.
  I will declare his might to him who fares downstream
  And to him who fares upstream.

[1] Brit. Mus. Stela No. 589.
[2] Gunn's translation, almost untouched.   [3] Berlin Stela 20377.

Be ye ware of him:
Herald him to son and daughter,
To great and small.
Declare ye him to generations and generations
That have not yet come into being.
Declare him to the fishes in the stream
And to the birds in the heaven.
Herald him to him that knows him not and to him that knows
*   him.*
Be ye ware of him.
Thou art Amun, the lord of him that is silent.
Who comest at the call of the humble.
I called upon thee when I was in distress,
And thou didst come that thou mightest save me.
That thou mightest give breath to him that was wretched,
That thou mightest save me that was in bondage.
Thou art Amun, Lord of Thebes,
That savest even him who is in the Underworld,
For thou art he who is [merciful?]
If one calls upon thee,
And thou art he who comes from afar.

Later in the same inscription occur the words:

He [1] said:
Though the servant was disposed to do evil
Yet is the Lord disposed to be merciful.
The Lord of Thebes spendeth not a whole day wroth;
His wrath is as the passing of a moment and naught is left.[2]
His wind is turned to us again in mercy;
Amun turns with his air.
As thy soul endureth mayest thou be merciful;
May we not again suffer that which has been averted!

This is a type of literature which has remarkably close

---

[1] I. e. Nebre, the dedicator of the stela.
[2] Cf. Psalms, 103. 9: 'He will not always chide: neither will he keep his anger for ever.'

parallels in both Palestine and Mesopotamia. For Palestine it is easy to find examples from the Psalms, for instance the fifty-first, which begins:

> *Have mercy upon me, O God, according to thy loving-kindness:*
> *according unto the multitude of thy tender mercies blot out*
> *my transgressions.*
> *Wash me throughly from mine iniquity, and cleanse me from my*
> *sin.*
> *For I acknowledge my transgressions: and my sin is ever before me.*

From Babylonia we may take an instance which in feeling has one essential difference from both the examples quoted, for the singer, while he prays the god to turn away his wrath, professes to be ignorant of the nature of his offence. It begins as follows:

> *O that the rage in the heart of the Lord might be appeased!*
> *May the god whom I know not be appeased,*
> *May the goddess whom I know not be appeased!*

Later we find the profession of innocence:

> *The sin which I have done know I not,*
> *And I am not aware of my transgression.*

The rest is much more in the style of the Egyptian and Hebrew examples.

> *In the wrath of his heart the lord hath looked banefully on me;*
> *In the fierceness of his heart the god hath smitten me with his enmity:*
> *The goddess hath been wroth with me and made me like to a sick*
> *man.*
> *The god whom I know and whom I know not hath oppressed me;*
> *The goddess whom I know and whom I know not hath caused me*
> *to suffer.*
> *When I sought help none took me by the hand;*
> *When I cry aloud no man hearkens to me.*
> *I turn me to my merciful god, I cry aloud to him;*
> *I embrace and I kiss the feet of my goddess.*
> *O Lord, cast not thy bondman down;*
> *Seize him by the hand as he lies in the miry water.*

The sin that I have committed turn into good,
Let the wind bear away my transgressions;
  Take from me like a garment the multitude of my iniquities.
My god, though my sins be seven times seven, yet wash away my sins.

It is clear that in all three countries this type of penitential psalm had a certain vogue. While, however, in Egypt it is known to us only from a restricted [1] group of stelae, all of much the same date, in Palestine and Babylonia it was recognized as a definite type of literature, and collections of such psalms were made. The Hebrew examples are the latest in date, but in literary merit they far surpass the others. In no branch of literature do the Hebrews establish a more definite superiority than in this.

Not the least remarkable phenomenon of Egyptian literature consists in the collections of love-songs which have come down to us from the New Empire. Three such collections are known to us, one from the Papyrus Harris 500 in the British Museum, one from a papyrus in Turin, and another from a papyrus in private ownership not yet published. The London papyrus contains several groups of songs. One of these is called *The lovely delightful songs of thy sister whom thy heart loveth, when she cometh from the meadow.* As elsewhere in oriental love-songs the lovers call themselves sister and brother. Here is an excerpt: [2]

[1] This restriction must surely be a matter of accident. The humble persons who dedicated these stelae certainly did not compose these admirable poems, which must be excerpts, altered to suit the occasion, from works well known at the time. I have always felt that Gunn went too far when he called his article (above quoted) *The Religion of the Poor*, and that Breasted was overbold when, in his clever *Development of Religion and Thought in Ancient Egypt* (London, n.d.), he labelled the period to which these stelae belong 'The Age of Personal Piety', mainly on the ground of their existence.

[2] *Egyptian Hieratic Papyri in the British Museum*, Second Series, Pls. XLIII–XLIV. I regret that I have been unable to collate the original and have consequently been obliged to work from the photographic reproductions.

*My beloved brother, my heart burneth for thy love . . . I say to thee,
Behold what I do. I am come to catch, with my trap in my hand and
my cage . . . All the birds of Punt settle upon Egypt, anointed with
myrrh. The one that cometh first it taketh my worm. Its odour
comes from Punt, its claws are full of myrrh.*

*How I long for thee, that we might take it out together, I alone
with thee, that thou mightest hear the shrill cry of my myrrh-
anointed one!*

*How good it were if thou shouldest be with me when I set the trap!
Most lovely is it to go to the meadow unto him who is beloved.*

*The voice of the goose caught on its worm crieth out, but love of
thee holdeth me back that I cannot release it. I will take away my
nets. 'How then,' my mother will say, to whom I go each evening
laden with birds, 'hast thou set no trap to-day?' Thy love hath
carried me off. . . .*

*I see sweet cake and it is as salt, and mead, which is sweet in the
mouth, is like the gall of birds. The breath of thy nostrils is that
alone which maketh my heart to live. I have found that Amun is
given to me thereby for ever and ever.*

In the next group of songs, called Songs of Pastime, the
maiden is in the garden and is perhaps making a garland of
flowers. The names of the various plants one after another
suggest, each by means of a pun, some thought concerning
the beloved, which she then expresses in a few sentences.[1]

There are saamu-*flowers in it. One is uplifted in their presence.
I am thy first sister. I am unto thee like the acre which I have planted
with flowers and all manner of sweet-smelling herbs; and in it is a
pool which thy hand hath digged, in the cool of the north wind, a
lovely place where I walk, thine hand upon mine, and my body
satisfied and my heart glad at our going together. It is mead to me to
hear thy voice, and I live because I hear it. If I but see thee it is
better to me than eating and drinking.*

In the Turin papyrus, which unfortunately is very fragmentary and very difficult, the various trees of the orchard

---

[1] *Op. cit.*, Pl. XLVI.

speak, inviting the maiden and her beloved to dally in their shade.[1]

[The . . . tree] speaks. My stones are like unto her teeth, the form of my fruit is like unto her breasts. [I am the kindest] of the orchard, for I abide at every season, that the sister may dally with her brother, . . . drunk with wine and mead, and anointed with oil of kemi. [The other trees] all pass away, save me alone in the garden: I pass twelve months [of the year] standing, though the bloom has fallen; that of last year is still within me. I am the first. The others say, Behold, we are but second.

But if it happen again I will not keep silent for them, [I will tell] it, that the offence may be seen and punishment done unto the beloved one, that so she may not [wreathe] her staves with lotus, with flowers . . . and buds. Ointment . . . beer of every kind. May she cause thee to pass the day merrily. A tent of rushes is a sheltered spot. Behold, he has truly come forth. Come, that we may cajole him. Let him spend the whole day . . . .

The fig tree utters its voice. Its foliage comes saying, [I will] be a servant to the mistress. Is there any so noble as I? Yet if thou hast no slave I am the servant [brought from] Syria as booty for the beloved. She caused me to be set in her orchard. She poured no [water for me], yet I spend the whole day drinking. . . . As my soul lives, O beloved one, mayst thou cause me to be brought into thy presence.

The little sycamore which she planted with her own hand. It utters its voice to speak. Verily the . . . is sweet as the foam of honey. How lovely are its beautiful branches(?), green . . . ! It is laden with clusters of fruit. It is redder than jasper. Its leaves are like turquoise, polished(?) like glass. Its wood is like the colour of neshmet-stone, its grain(?) like the besbes-tree. It draws to itself them that have no shade, so cool is its shadow. It gives a letter into the hand of a little maid, daughter of its gardener. It bids her hasten to the beloved, Come that thou mayest pass a moment in . . . A booth and a tent house thee. My gardeners rejoice and make merry at seeing thee. Send thy slaves before thee equipped with their gear. One is

[1] Pleyte-Rossi, *Papyrus de Turin* (Leyden, 1869–76), Pls. LXXIX–LXXXII. The papyrus is both defective and corrupt.

*drunk with running to thee ere yet one has drunk. Thy servants come,
bearing their utensils. They bring beer of every kind and all manner
of bread mixed(?) and many fruits of yesterday and to-day, and every
kind of delicious fruit. Come that thou mayest spend the day in
merriment day after day for three days, sitting in my shade. Her
lover is at her right hand. She makes him drunken, yielding to his
request. The feast is disordered with drunkenness; yet she remains
with her brother. The . . . is spread beneath me(?) while the sister
is at her walking about. But I am discreet to tell not what I see.
I will speak no word.*

The kindness of Professor Alan Gardiner enables me to
quote from his translation[1] of the love-songs in the Chester
Beatty Papyrus No. 1, which he is engaged in publishing.
Here is a charming little poem which embodies an ingenious
thought neatly worked out:

*It is seven days yesterday since I saw the sister,
And sickness encroaches upon me;
I am become heavy in my members,
And have no awareness of mine own body.
If the master-physicians come to me
My heart has no comfort of their remedies;
The magicians have no resource,
And my sickness is not discerned.
That which I have told alone can revive me,
Her name it is that can raise me up.
The coming and going of her messengers
Is that which revives my heart.
Better for me is the sister than any medicine,
More important is she for me than all the book of remedies;
Her coming in is my health.
When I see her then shall I be well,
If she open her eye my limbs shall recover their youth;*

[1] Dr. Gardiner warns me that his translation is subject to revision.
I quote it as it stands, with only such small verbal modifications as to
bring it into line with certain conventions which I have tried to observe
throughout these lectures.

If she speak I shall be strong.
When I embrace her it drives evil from me,
And it passes away for seven days.

Here are two excerpts from another song portraying the impatience of the maid for the coming of her lover.[1]

O that thou mayest come to the sister quickly like a royal messenger whose lord is impatient for his message, and his heart is fain to hear it; even a messenger for whom all the stables have been harnessed, and he has horses at the halting-places, and the chariot is ready yoked in its place, and there is no rest for him upon the road. He reaches the house of the sister, and his heart rejoices.

O that thou mayest come like a steed of the king, choicest of a thousand of all the principal stallions(?) of the stables! It is distinguished from the others in its food, and its lord knows its paces. If it hear the sound of the whip it knows no delay, and there is no chief of the cavalry who can come level with it. How well the sister knows that he is not far distant from the sister!

Those who have previously been unacquainted with the Egyptian love-songs will certainly be astonished at the freshness and variety of these examples, which are chosen quite at random, and do not illustrate by any means all the various forms which this type of poem took under the New Empire.

From Babylonia literally nothing of this kind has come down to us. The parallel with the Song of Songs which is Solomon's, however, scarcely needs pointing out. In both cases we have poems which are not merely erotic but which breathe a strong love of nature, and which depend for their effect on the comparison between the beauties of the beloved person and those of natural objects, more particularly of trees, flowers, and gardens. Once again, however, as in the hymns, we are struck by the wider range of imagination in the Hebrew work and by the more sustained quality of its outbursts. Yet the poet's conception of a love-lyric is in both

[1] Again from Pap. Chester Beatty, No. 1.

cases precisely the same. It is not my duty to suggest that the Hebrew songs are based on Egyptian originals; no doubt both belong to a type of poetry common to the Near East in general, despite our failure so far to find a trace of it in Babylonia. I would nevertheless remind you that the Egyptian songs, even in their present form, date from 1200 B.C., whereas the Hebrew book can hardly be older than 400 B.C.

If the Egyptians were the inventors of the love-poem, and it is not unlikely that, with their love of brightness and gaiety, they were, we may well regard it as one of their chief contributions to literature. The young poets of our post-war period may devise a form of love-poetry so new and bizarre as to have no point of contact with this early product, but it may safely be affirmed that up to the present no poet has written of love without saying many things which his Egyptian forerunners thought and said three thousand years ago.

Our comparative survey of the achievement of these three early nations in the field of lyric poetry may be very rapidly summed up as follows. The Hebrews, in the last few centuries before Christ, produced a quality and quantity of lyric poetry both sacred and profane with which neither Egypt nor Babylonia can compete. At the same time these two countries, at a much earlier date, had between them made highly successful experiments in every part of the field in which the Hebrews afterwards surpassed them. To the credit of Babylonia may be set the development up to a high point of aesthetic excellence of hymns to deities, of prayers in lyric form, and of psalms of penitence. Egypt, while apparently achieving less in the two latter genres, produced some admirable hymns to her gods and songs of victory to her kings, and gave to the world what are, so far as we know, its earliest love-poems.

LECTURE III

WE now come to the third main division of early
writing, namely wisdom-literature. And here it is
that, in my opinion, Egypt achieved her highest literary
distinction. In this genre Babylonia has left us comparatively little. Palestine, on the other hand, attempted much
and achieved much. Proverbs, Ecclesiastes, The Wisdom
of Solomon, Ecclesiasticus, and the more didactic Psalms at
once spring to our minds; and the Book of Job and certain
portions of the prophetic literature may be assigned to the
same class.

In Egypt this wisdom-literature may conveniently be
divided into two classes, the didactic and the contemplative.
To the first class are to be assigned a number of papyri
which contain what purport to be Instructions, given
generally by a father to his son.[1] These consist of series of
maxims, sometimes of purely worldly wisdom, more rarely
of real ethical value. The specimens of this literature which
have survived can mostly be traced back at least to the
XIIth Dynasty, but the genre undoubtedly had its roots in
the Old Kingdom, as we shall shortly see. The other class
of wisdom-literature I have called contemplative, rather for
want of a better name than because the label in all cases fits
accurately. It seems to have arisen in or just after the dis-
astrous years which followed the fall of the Old Kingdom,
a time of internal confusion and foreign invasion, when
the Egyptians realized with horror that not even the bodies
of the kings beneath their vast pyramids were immune from
violation. In the literary field these events seem to have
taken effect in a pessimistic outbreak, chiefly characterized

---

[1] This parental form of instruction, if I may so call it, has not found
favour with the modern moralistic writers. Early in the thirteenth
century, however, a certain Herr von Windsbach, known as 'the Wins-
beke', wrote for his son's instruction an exposition of chivalrous
morality in a poem of fifty-six stanzas.

by vivid descriptions of the appalling state of Egypt and the futility of life, together with prophecies of better things.

These two types of literature must be considered separately. The didactic form is represented by four important documents and some lesser ones. The four are the Proverbs of Ptahhotep, the Instruction of Dwauf, the Instruction of King Amenemhet, and the Instruction for King Merikere.

The Proverbs of Ptahhotep are known to us from three papyri, two dating from the XIIth Dynasty and the other much later,[1] but it seems probable that, just as some of the biblical Proverbs may really go back to Solomon, so some of the wise sayings of Egypt may really have been uttered by the famous vizier Ptahhotep of the Vth Dynasty. In the papyrus this vizier is represented as begging the king to allow him to make for himself a 'staff of old age', i.e. officially to appoint his son as his successor, and to formulate for him a series of rules of conduct. The king agrees and Ptahhotep delivers his aphorisms. They cover wide ground, but on the whole it may be said that they are intended rather for one who is to hold high office in the state than for the ordinary man. There is practically no arrangement, the orator passing from one subject to another quite abruptly, and ending with a long coda on the usefulness of his teaching and the necessity of passing it on from generation to generation. This lack of order must be regarded as a literary defect, but it is one that is to some extent shared by the various sections of the Old Testament Book of Proverbs. It is most important to notice that the Egyptian work is not merely consciously literary in character, but openly prides itself on being so. The maxims are said to be useful, but they are

---

[1] Papyrus Prisse and Papyrus British Museum 10371 + 10435 are of XIIth-Dynasty date; Pap. B.M. 10509 is very much later. There is also a fragment on a scribe's writing-tablet found by Lord Carnarvon in 1909. For a complete parallel text see E. Dévaud, *Les Maximes de Ptahhotep*, Fribourg, 1916. There are partial translations in all the books on Egyptian literature, but a rendering embodying the results of recent research in Egyptian grammar and lexicography is badly needed.

also definitely stated to be beautifully expressed, and Ptahhotep claims to instruct not only in conduct but in the rules
of elegant diction.

The importance of this work in the history of the world's
literature makes it worth while to quote from it at some
length. It is perhaps the most difficult of all Middle
Kingdom papyri to translate—the variants in the later
papyrus show that the Egyptians of the New Empire themselves found it far from easy—and I have therefore chosen
for quotation those sections whose meaning is most certain.
Over each passage I insert for the reader's help a title giving
its subject.

Intellectual snobbery

*Be not arrogant because of thy knowledge, and be not puffed up for
that thou art a learned man. Take counsel with the ignorant as with
the learned, for the limits of art cannot be reached, and no artist is
perfect in his excellence.[1] Goodly discourse is more hidden than the
precious green-stone, and yet it is found with slave-girls over the
millstones.*

Righteousness in leaders

*If thou be a leader, ruling the multitude, strive after every excel-
lence, that thy conduct may be without fault. Great is righteousness, and its worth is abiding; it hath not been put to confusion since
the days of Osiris. But he that transgresseth its ordinances is
punished. It lieth as a path in front of the ignorant. Wrong-doing
hath never brought its venture safe to port.*

Conduct of guests at table

*If thou art a guest at the table of one who is greater than thou,
take what he may offer thee as it is set before thee. Fix thy gaze upon
what is before thee, and pierce not thy host with many glances, for it
is an abomination to force thy notice upon him. Speak not to him
until he biddeth thee, for one knoweth not what may be offensive; but*

[1] I. e. the fool may sometimes supply a piece of information which
the wise man could not give.

speak when he addresseth thee, for so shall thy words give satisfaction.

Conduct of envoys

If thou art a confidant whom prince sendeth to prince, be strictly exact when he sendeth thee. Do his errand for him even as he telleth it. Beware of embittering with words that may incense(?) prince against prince. Hold fast to truth and transgress her not. Verily the satisfaction of a grudge is not told to a man's credit. Quarrel with no man great or small, for that is an abomination.

Patience with suppliants

If thou art a leader be kind in hearing the speech of the suppliant. Treat him not roughly until he have unburdened himself of what he was minded to tell thee. The complainant setteth greater store by the easing of his mind than by the accomplishment of that for which he came.[1] As for him who dealeth roughly with supplication, men say of him 'Why, pray, hath he ignored it? Naught that men beg of him ever cometh to pass'. To listen kindly comforteth the heart.

Relations with women

If thou wouldst prolong friendship in a house where thou visitest as possessor, as brother or as friend, in whatsoever place thou frequentest beware of approaching the women. It is no fit place wherein to do it. There is no wisdom in the indulgence of lust, and a thousand men have been led aside from their good. A little moment, like to a dream, and death is the penalty for enjoying it.

Covetousness

If thou wouldst that thy conduct be good, keep thee from every evil. Beware of covetousness. It is the evil sickness of the bethu-worm.[2] *No man can consort therewith; it setteth division between fathers and mothers, and between brothers by the same mother. It parteth wife and*

---

[1] Truly Ptahhotep was a wise old man. So long as we may have our grumble we often care little whether the cause of it is removed or not.

[2] Known from the medical papyri; a parasite, causing incurable disease in man.

husband. It is a handful(?) of every evil, as it were a bag of every-
thing hateful. A man shall thrive if he be truly righteous. He who
followeth in his footsteps shall make for himself a fortune thereby.
But the covetous man shall have no tomb.

Marriage

If thou be wise marry. Love thy wife sincerely. Fill her belly and
clothe her back. Oil is the remedy for her body. Make glad her
heart all thy life. She is a profitable field for her lord.

Conduct in council

If thou be a wise man sitting in the council of his lord, confine thy
heart to what is good and be silent, for it is more valuable than the
teftef-plant. Speak only when thou knowest that thou canst resolve
the doubt. He who giveth good counsel is an artist, for speech is more
difficult than any craft.

Behaviour in changed circumstances

If thou be great that once wast humble, and rich that aforetime
wast poor, in the city that thou knowest, be not close(?) because of
that which happened to thee of old. Be not overcareful in respect of
thy wealth, which hath come to thee by the god's gift. Thou shalt not
lag behind another like thee to whom the like hath come to pass.

Treatment of official superiors

Bend thy back to him that is over thee, to thy superior in the
administration; thy house shall abide by reason of his substance, and
thy recompense shall come in due season. Evil is he who resisteth his
superior, for one liveth only so long as he [1] *is gracious.*

Towards the end of the document occurs a passage which
I quote as an example of the curious love of the Egyptians
for puns, or, to be exact, for playing with numbers of words
derived from the same root. The root here used is the verb
sōtem to hear, and an ingenuity as remarkable as it is misplaced is shown in combining, within the limits of sense,

[1] The superior.

every possible noun, adjective, and verbal form derivable from this root.[1]

Exhortation to hearken

Profitable is hearing to a son who hears. The hearer entereth as one who has heard, and he who heareth becometh a hearer, good at hearing and good at speaking. He who heareth is a lord of profit, for hearing is profitable to the hearer. Hearing is better than any thing, for thereby ariseth goodly love. How good it is that the son should hearken when his father speaketh! He shall reach old age by reason of it. He who heareth is beloved of the god, but he who is hated of the gods heareth not. It is the heart that mouldeth its lord as one who heareth or as one who heareth not. A man's heart is his life-prosperity-and-health. How good it is that a son should hearken unto his father! How glad is he to whom men say, 'A son whose virtue is that of a master who heareth'! As for the hearer to whom it is said, he is virtuous from birth, an honoured one in the sight of his father, and his remembrance is in the mouths of the living that are upon earth so long as they live.

As for the fool who heareth not, he shall have no success. He regardeth knowledge as ignorance and good as evil. He maketh himself to be blamed daily for the doing of all that is hateful. He liveth upon that by which men die. To speak evil is the food of his mouth. His character therefore is known to the magistrates, and he dieth a living death each day. Men will have naught to do with him by reason of the multitude of evils that are upon him daily.

The Instruction of Dwauf is addressed by Dwauf son of Khety to his son Pepi, whom he was taking up the river to the capital, where he was to study in the writing-school for the career of a scribe. The work exalts this profession above all others, and constitutes what has not been unaptly named a Satire on the Professions. It certainly dates from the

---

[1] Ptahhotep might reply that even Shakespeare thought the device not beneath his dignity:

> For wisdom's sake, a word that all men love,
> Or for love's sake, a word that loves all men.

Love's Labour's Lost, Act IV, Sc. iii, ll. 357–8.

We do not, however, reckon such passages among Shakespeare's noblest.

beginning of the Middle Kingdom, as the personal names in it show, but it is known to us only from schoolboys' copies made—and made, alas! very inaccurately—in the schools of the New Empire. The work was clearly very popular in these schools, for excerpts from it occur in various papyri and also on ostraca. Two papyri indeed, those known as Sallier II and Anastasi VII, both in the British Museum, actually contain parts or the whole of the same three compositions, the Instruction of Dwauf, the Instruction of Amenemhet (see below) and the Hymn to the Nile. The following quotations will illustrate the scope and style of the work:

Set thy heart on books. . . . Would that I might make thee to love books more than thy mother, that I might put their beauty before thine eyes. It [1] is greater than any profession.

Never have I seen the stone-worker sent on an embassy or the goldsmith despatched on an errand. But I have seen the coppersmith at his task at the mouth of his furnace. His fingers were like the hide(?) of crocodiles; he stank more than eggs or fish.

Here follow descriptions of the hard fate of the carpenter, the barber, the fletcher, the fisherman, the gardener and others, but the copies are so corrupt that continuous quotation is impossible. The lesson of the whole is contained in one sentence:

Behold there is no calling wherein a man hath no master save that of the scribe, and he is himself the master.

This theme was considerably elaborated as time went on, and from other manuscripts of the New Empire which do not definitely profess to give us the composition of Dwauf himself we have fuller descriptions of the hardships of the various callings. Here, for example, is the picture of the life of the husbandman: [2]

I am told that thou dost forsake writing and give thyself up to

[1] The scribe's career.
[2] Pap. Sallier I, 6.1 ff. = Pap. Anastasi V, 15. 6 ff.

P

pleasures. Wilt thou not bethink thee how it fareth with the husband-man when the harvest cometh to be registered? The worm hath taken half his corn, the hippopotamus the rest. Mice abound in the field, and the locust hath descended. The cattle devour and the sparrows pilfer. Alas for the husbandman!

The remainder that lieth upon the threshing-floor, the thieves have made away with it. The ploughshare(?) of copper hath perished, and the yoke of horses hath died at the threshing and ploughing.

And now the scribe landeth upon the embankment to register the harvest. His bodyguard carry sticks and his negroes palm-switches. They cry, Give up your corn. And there is none there. He is stretched out and beaten, he is bound and thrown into the canal. His wife is bound before his eyes and his children put in fetters. His neighbours run away to look after their own corn.

But the scribe, he directeth the work of all men. For him there are no taxes, for he payeth tribute in writing, and there are no dues for him. Do thou mark it.

Equally admirable is the description of the life of the soldier: [1]

Come let me tell thee of the woes of the soldier; how that his masters are many, the general, the troop-commander, the major, the standard-bearer, the lieutenant, the scribe, the captain of fifty, the platoon-commander. They go in and out of their offices in the palace. They say 'Produce the man that can work'. He is awakened when but an hour hath gone, and driven about like a donkey. He worketh till the sun setteth, bringing the darkness of night. He is hungry, his body is worn out, he is dead while yet alive. He receiveth his corn ration when he is released from duty, but it is uneatable when ground.

He is called up for Syria. He hath no comfort; there are nei-ther clothes nor sandals, for the war-equipment is being gathered at the fortress of Tharu.[2] He marcheth high up in the mountains. He drinketh water but once in three days, and then it is brackish and

---

[1] A free rendering of Pap. Lansing, 9. 4 ff.

[2] A frontier fortress in the north-east of the Delta, and the base for operations in Syria. The point seems to be that the clothes are in store at Tharu instead of being available for distribution to the troops when needed.

tasteth like salt. His body is broken with dysentery. Then cometh the enemy and encompasseth him round about with arrows, and life is far from him. They say to him 'Forward, brave soldier, win for thyself a good name.' But he is half unconscious, his knees are loosed, and his head paineth him.

When the victory cometh his majesty handeth over the captives to be taken down to Egypt. A foreign woman is faint with marching; she is laid upon the neck of the soldier. His haversack falleth and others pick it up, while he is bowed down beneath the weight of the Syrian woman. In his village are his wife and children, but he dieth and doth not reach it.

Be a scribe, and save thee from the soldier's fate. Shouldest thou cry out there will ever be one to cry 'Here am I' and to save thee from a beating.

This idea, the comparison of the various occupations, is a commonplace in the literature of most nations. Yet the Egyptians were the first to attempt it, and they not only attempted it, they succeeded in it.

The Instructions of King Amenemhet I to his son Senusret,[1] who afterwards succeeded him, deserve attention for the note of bitterness which runs through them. An attempt had been made on the king's life by men whom he trusted, and in consequence his counsel to his son is mainly one of suspicion and mistrust.

When thou sleepest, he says, *do thou thyself guard thine heart, for in the day of trouble a man hath no adherents. I gave to the poor and reared the orphan, I caused him that was naught to reach the goal even as him that was of account.*

It was he who ate my food that abused me, it was he to whom I had given my hand that aroused fear therewith. They that clothed them in my fine linen looked upon me as a shadow, they that anointed themselves with my frankincense defiled me while covered with it. My images are among the living and my portions among men; yet they made an attempt against me without its being heard, and a violent deed of arms without its being seen.

[1] See Griffith in *Zeitschr. für ägyptische Sprache*, xxxiv, pp. 35 ff.

More important than this is the Instruction for Merikere.[1] It was spoken by a king of the IXth or Xth Dynasty, whose name is lost, to his son Merikere. The advice given covers a wide field. In part it is political, and concerns the treatment of the rival House of Thebes, which at this time held half of Upper Egypt, as well as the policy of defence against the dangerous Syrians on the north-east. This political section is combined with more general advice suited to a future king, and exhortations to righteousness breathing a high moral and, curious to relate, a strong monotheistic tone. The maxims are here not thrown together at random as in Ptahhotep, but arranged in logical fashion, and the work is thus superior to Ptahhotep in the literary as well as in the ethical sense; in fact it may be classed with the Dialogue of a Man with his Soul and the Prophecy of Neferrohu among the finest works of Egyptian literature.

Do justice, says the king, *that thou mayest endure upon earth. Calm the weeper. Oppress not the widow. Expel no man from the possessions of his father. Degrade not magistrates from their posts. Take heed lest thou punish wrongfully. Slaughter not, for it doth not profit thee. . . . God knoweth the froward, and God requiteth his sins in blood.*

As for the Magistrates who judge sinners, mark thee that they will not be lenient on that day of judging miserable men in the hour of performing their function. Woe to him who is accused as one conscious of sin! Put not thy faith in length of years, for they regard a lifetime as but an hour. A man surviveth after reaching the haven of death, and for sole treasure there are laid beside him his deeds. Eternal is the existence yonder, and he who hath made light of it is a fool. But as for him who hath reached it without wrongdoing, he shall continue yonder like a god, stepping forward boldly like the Lords of Eternity.

In reading this combination of political advice and exhortations to righteousness it is impossible not to be re-

---

[1] *Journ. Eg. Arch.*, i, pp. 20 ff.

minded of the Hebrew prophets, whose writings form such
an important part of the Old Testament. And this is perhaps
the time and place to remark that the phenomenon of the
prophets is one to which there is no true parallel in Egypt.
This race of patriots, convinced that the political troubles
of their country were the consequences of its wickedness,
anxious to impress their countrymen with their own lofty
conception of deity and of righteousness, stands alone in the
history of the ancient world.[1] Yet the superficial resemblance between the Instruction for Merikere and the Book
of Amos, for instance, is one which cannot fail to strike the
reader, and there is an astonishing parallel between the
incomplete monotheism of Amos and that of the Instructions.[2] Whereas, however, the successors of Amos sub-
limated his conception until it became a true monotheism,
the idea seems to have undergone no further development
in Egypt. The essential difference between the two works in
form is that in Amos political misfortune is treated as the
result of iniquity and a call to righteousness is issued, while
in Merikere the aim is not to assign the cause for a disaster
but to show how righteousness, coupled with reasonable
worldly precautions, leads to political success.

I cannot leave the consideration of this portion of the
Egypt's wisdom-literature without speaking of the newly
discovered Proverbs of Amenope, which have attained such
notoriety as the reputed source of parts of the biblical
Proverbs. Apart from their remarkable textual correspon-
dences with the text of Proverbs, their chief interest lies in
the fact that they are a late composition, hardly earlier than
the beginning of the first millennium B.C.; this shows that the
Egyptians were still producing literature of this kind at the
very time when, owing to the conquests of the Ramessides,
Egyptian influence in Syria was strongest. Even if it be true
that nothing in the Hebrew wisdom-books was written

---

[1] See T. H. Robinson, *Prophecy and the Prophets* (London, 1925), and
bibliography (by A. S. Peake) there given.

[2] The god of the Instructions is clearly the sun-god.

down until several centuries after this, the new papyrus
nevertheless brings the two literatures nearer together in
time, and indicates the period at which Egyptian wisdom
may have made its chief impression on the Hebrews.

From the moment of its publication the new papyrus
attracted the notice of Biblical scholars owing to the verbal
identity of some of its aphorisms with those of the Proverbs.
That the author of the latter had been acquainted with the
work of Amenope seemed certain when Erman suggested
that the word שלשום in Prov. xxii. 20, which had puzzled
all the commentators, and of which the most diverse translations had been given, bore its ordinary sense of 'thirty' and
referred to the thirty chapters into which Amenope's Proverbs were divided.[1] This view has since been modified by
Sellin and Gressmann, who, while accepting Erman's
translation, take the word to refer to the thirty subsections,
of roughly four verses each, into which the third section of
Proverbs seems to be divisible.[2]

Though not free from difficulties this document is the
most perfect and the most translatable of all the Egyptian
wisdom-books. It is in metrical form, each chapter consisting of a group of from two to eleven stanzas, each stanza
containing four, more rarely two, strophes. Its advice
covers almost the whole field of behaviour, from the treatment of the old and infirm to the use of correct weights in
trade. Here is the chapter on over-anxiety:

> *Lay thee not down at night fearing the morrow,*
> *When day dawns what is the morrow like?*
> *Man knoweth not how the morrow may be.*
> (This line is lost.)
>
> *God is ever efficient,*
> *But man faileth ever.*

[1] *Sitzungsber. der preussischen Akad. der Wissenschaften*, phil.-hist. Klasse,
xv(1924), pp. 86 ff.

[2] Sellin in *Deutsche Literaturzeitung*, 1924, pp. 1325 ff. and 1873 ff.;
Gressmann in *Zeitschr. für die alttestamentliche Wissenschaft*, 1924,
pp. 272 ff.

The words that men say are one thing,
 The things that God doeth are another.

Say not 'There is no evil in me'
 And yet busy thyself in seeking strife.
For evil belongeth to God,[1]
 It is sealed with his finger.

There is no success with God,
 Nor is there failure before him;[2]
If man turn him to seek success,
 In a moment he destroyeth it.

Be resolute of heart, make firm thy mind,
 Steer not with thy tongue;
The tongue of a man is the rudder of the boat
 But the Lord of all is its pilot.

I refrain from further quotation, but refer the reader to Professor Griffith's admirable translation and to Canon Simpson's treatment of the parallels with the Book of Proverbs.[3] The great importance of the composition from the comparative point of view will be evident to all who read it. The width of its scope, its high moral tone, and its poetical form, all bring it nearer to Hebrew literature than perhaps any other document which has survived from ancient Egypt.

And lastly a word as to the Maxims of Ani. Up to the present this has been published only from a corrupt copy made by a schoolboy of the XXIInd Dynasty, but fragments of another copy in the Louvre show that the text is somewhat older than this. I quote a few passages which contain shrewd counsels expressed with great freshness.

The temple of God abhorreth loud crying. Pray with a loving

---

[1] God alone is the judge of evil and good.
[2] Earthly success and failure do not count with God.
[3] *Journ. Eg. Arch.*, xii, pp. 191 ff. and 232 ff.

heart whose words are all secret. So shall he accomplish thy desire; he shall hear thy prayer and accept thine offering.

Harm not thyself by the drinking of beer. When thou wouldst speak, a different utterance cometh forth from thy mouth. If thou fallest and breakest a limb there is none to stretch out a hand to thee. Thy boon companions cry, 'Defend me from this fellow when he drinketh.' And if one cometh to seek thee and to question thee, thou art found lying on the ground, and art as a little child.

Sit not while one standeth that is older than thou.

If thou take to thyself a wife and settle in thine own house, keep before thee how thy mother gave thee birth and all her bringing up of thee likewise. Give her no occasion to find fault with thee or to lift up her voice to God, that he might hear her cry.

Eat no bread when another is in want without stretching out thy hand to him with bread. One is wealthy, another is in want. He that last year was rich is now a groom. The course wherein the water ran last year is changed and this year it taketh another course. Great oceans have become dry land and banks have become an abyss.

The examples which have here been given of the didactic literature of the Ancient Egyptians from Ptahhotep to Amenope cover a period of nearly fifteen hundred years, and this period might have been extended by another millennium had I included the Demotic Papyrus Insinger, which dates from the first half-century after Christ. Of this type of literature the Egyptians seem on present evidence to have been the inventors. We can trace its history from the crude and formless utterances of Ptahhotep to the finished stanzas of Amenope.

There is, however, just one piece of evidence to show that this kind of composition was not wholly unknown in Babylonia. It is a text of which Assurbanipal's library has yielded two versions, while a third, written in neo-Babylonian, is also known.[1] It is a collection of aphorisms

---

[1] Langdon, *Babylonian Wisdom*, pp. 88 ff.

addressed to 'my son'. A fragment of what appears to be the
same work, found at Ashur, contains a reference to Utnapishtim, the Babylonian hero of the Flood, and it has therefore been suggested that these Instructions were represented
as being given by Utnapishtim to his sons after the Flood.
If this were proved correct, and if, further, Langdon is
right[1] in assuming a Sumerian origin for this composition,
Babylonia would challenge Egypt's claim to be the inventor
of this particular type of wisdom-literature. There is, however, little to be gained by speculation on the point, which
may be settled at any moment by excavation. In the meantime, while keeping an open mind, we can safely say that up
to the present Egypt's claim to priority in this branch of
composition is still a strong one.[2]

These Babylonian aphorisms have much in common in
content with those of Palestine and Egypt, as indeed any
aphorisms of general application must have. It is interesting
to find among them *Unto him that doeth thee evil shalt thou
return good.*

The best preserved passage runs thus:

> *Slander not, but speak kindliness.*
> > *Speak no evil, but say that which is good.*
> *He that slandereth and speaketh evil*
> > *Shamash shall recompense, . . . ing his head.*
> *Open not wide thy mouth, keep guard over thy lips.*
> > *When thou art aroused speak not at once;*
> *If thou speak too quickly thou shalt repent it hereafter;*
> > *Calm thy mind with silence.*
> *Daily bring unto thy god offering*
> > *Of sacrifice, prayer and most acceptable incense.*
> *Keep a pure heart before thy god;*
> > *This it is that is most acceptable to the deity.*

---

[1] *Op. cit.*, p. 89.

[2] We can hardly class as literature the collection of proverbs made in
Sumerian and Babylonian for Assurbanipal's library. See Weber, *Lit.*,
pp. 306–7.

Prayer and supplication and prostration
  Shalt thou offer him each morning, and thy power shall be
      great;
They shall win for thee the uttermost with God.
In thy wisdom learn from the tablet;
  Fear of the god begetteth favour;
Offering lengtheneth life,
  And prayer washeth away sin.

We must now pass to the second class of Egyptian wisdom-literature, that which I have, for want of a better name, called contemplative.

This is almost entirely a product of the disasters which followed the downfall of the Old Kingdom to which reference has been made above, and is essentially pessimistic. Four works call for notice, the Dispute of a Man with his Soul, the Admonitions of Ipuwer, the Complaint of Khakhe-perresenb, and the Prophecies of Neferrohu.

The first of these, known variously to Egyptologists as The Man weary of Life, The Suicide, and The Dispute of a Man with his Soul, is contained in a papyrus of XIIth-Dynasty date, and there is no evidence that the composition of the piece is definitely earlier than this. In the minds of many of us it is the masterpiece of Egyptian literature, a work almost worthy to be regarded as a masterpiece of literature generally.

The subject of this poem, for poem it is, though probably not metrical in form throughout, is a discussion between a man and his *ba*, which, though commonly rendered 'soul', would appear to mean 'external manifestation' or something of that kind, and which is, for the purposes of the present poem, regarded as a separate entity from the man, though not wholly independent of him. Owing to the loss of the opening lines the exact setting of the discussion is not quite clear. It would seem, however, that the dead man is standing before his judges in the next world and explaining to them a dispute which he had had with his *ba* on earth.

He had wished to commit suicide, apparently by fire, and the *ba* had opposed this, on grounds too complicated to be discussed here. It draws his attention to the evils of death, for even those who could afford to build for themselves in red granite and to make for themselves beautiful pyramids can rely on receiving the necessary supplies of food and drink from their survivors no more than *the weary ones who die upon the river bank with none to care for them. And the water and the sun's heat alike destroy them, and the fishes of the river's bank have converse with them. Hearken unto me, Lo it is good for men to hearken. Enjoy thyself and forget care.*

This advice the *ba* follows up with two parables which are unfortunately very obscure. Then the man replies with a justification of his decision to destroy himself. This consists of four sections, each in metrical form. The first contains 8 verses, the second 16, the third 6 and the fourth 3. The form of these will at once appear from the following quotations.

The first poem describes how low the man's esteem on earth had fallen:

> *Behold my name stinks*
> *More than the odour of carrion birds*
> *On summer days when the heaven is hot.*
>
> *Behold my name stinks*
> *More than the odour of fishermen,*
> *And the shores of the pools they have fished.*
>
> *Behold my name stinks*
> *More than that of a woman*
> *Of whom slander has been spoken concerning a man.*

The second section describes in sixteen verses the degenerate condition of mankind as it appears to the suicide.

> *To whom should I speak today?*
> *Brothers are evil;*
> *The friends of today love not.*

To whom should I speak today?
Hearts are covetous;
Every man plundereth the goods of his fellow.

To whom should I speak today?
Yesterday is perished,
And violence is come upon all men.

To whom should I speak today?
The peaceful man is in evil case;
Good is cast aside everywhere.

To whom should I speak today?
Yesterday is forgotten;
Men do not as they were done by nowadays.

To whom should I speak today?
There is no heart of man
Whereon one might lean.

To whom should I speak today?
The righteous are no more;
The land is given over to evil-doers.

To whom should I speak today?
There is a lack of confidants;
Men have recourse to a stranger to tell their troubles.

To whom should I speak today?
I am heavy laden with misery,
And am without a comforter.

Next comes the third portion, which, for its beauty, I quote in full:

Death is in my eyes today
As when a sick man becomes whole,
As the walking abroad after illness.

Death is in my eyes today
Like the scent of myrrh,
Like sitting beneath the boat's sail on a breezy day.

Death is in my eyes today
Like the smell of water-lilies,
Like sitting on the bank of drunkenness.

Death is in my eyes today
Like a well-trodden road,
As when men return home from a foreign campaign.

Death is in my eyes today
Like the unveiling of the heaven,
As when a man attains there to that which he knew not.

Death is in my eyes today
Like the desire of a man to see his home
When he hath passed many years in captivity.

Shelley has said more wonderful things about death than this, but I question whether he or any one else has said anything more beautiful in its simplicity.

The fourth section deals with the happy state of the departed, but it is slightly obscure, and I prefer to end on the note struck by the third. The work finishes with a short passage in prose in which the *ba* affirms his readiness to follow the man to the next world if that be his desire.

The comparison with the Book of Job springs unasked into our minds. The settings are different. Job's misfortunes came from God and seemed to him undeserved. The Suicide's life-weariness is doubtless a reminiscence of the cruel days between the VIth and XIIth Dynasties. Job is shown to us in varying moods, or at least in varying phases of a mood, and in this sense the work is more elaborate than the Suicide. It is also more universal, for the Suicide, with its preconception of the *ba* and its relation to the man, and its dependence on Egyptian ideas of death and burial and the importance of the funerary rites as such, is highly local. Yet Job, especially in his calmer moments, reminds us forcibly of the suicide who longed for death at least fifteen hundred years before him.

The Admonitions of Ipuwer, known to us only from a

very corrupt XIXth-Dynasty copy on a papyrus in Leyden,[1] is another work which has its roots in the tragic days of the Early Intermediate Period. It would seem that in the opening paragraphs, which are lost, the king, appalled by the condition of the land, calls a council of his wise men and asks for their advice. A certain Ipuwer then proceeds to describe the disasters which had befallen Egypt, internal chaos, social revolution, decay of the authority of the magistrates and even of the king, foreign invasion and other horrors. Towards the end a hint is given as to how this situation may be redeemed, and of the happiness which may again be in store for Egypt. The work is rather elaborately constructed and consists of a prose framework in which are set six groups of verses.

Verily the Nile is in flood, yet no man plougheth for him.
  Every man saith, We know not what hath happened in the land.
Verily women are barren and there is no conception;
  Khnum fashioneth men no more by reason of the condition of the land.
Verily the children of princes are dashed against the walls;
  The children of desire are cast upon the desert;
  Khnum groaneth for very weariness.

Behold, he that possessed wealth now spendeth the night athirst;
  He that begged of him his dregs is now a possessor of bumpers.
Behold, they that possessed clothes are now in rags;
  He that wove not for himself now possesseth fine linen.
Behold, he that never built for himself a boat now possesseth ships;
  He that once possessed them beholdeth them, but they are his no more.
Behold, he that had no shade is now a possessor of shade;
  The possessors of shade are in the blast of the storm.
Behold, he that had no knowledge of the lyre now possesseth a harp;
  He to whom none sang now vaunteth the Goddess of Music.

[1] A. H. Gardiner, *The Admonitions of an Egyptian Sage*, Leipzig, 1909.

Behold, he that had no property is now a lord of wealth;
  The official speaketh praise of him.
Behold, the poor of the land have become rich;
  The possessor of property is now one who has naught.
Behold, [servants] have become masters of butlers;
  He who was a messenger now sends another.
Behold, he that had not a loaf is the possessor of a granary;
  His magazine is equipped with the goods of another.
Behold, he that was bald and had no oil
  Has become a possessor of jars of sweet myrrh.
Behold, she that had no box is now a possessor of furniture;
  She that beheld her face in water now possesseth a mirror.
Behold, noble ladies go hungry;
  What was prepared for them goes to sate the butchers.
Behold, cattle are left to stray, there is none to herd them;
  Each man must fetch for himself those that are branded with his
    name.
Behold, he that had no yoke of oxen is now a possessor of herds;
  He that could not find for himself oxen for ploughing is a possessor
    of droves.
Behold, he that had no grain is a possessor of granaries;
  He that fetched for himself rations now sends them forth.

Such is the style of this composition, a fine piece of imaginative poetry, which we should place even higher than we do did not corruptions and lacunae conceal so much of its meaning from us. The most astonishing thing about it is the close parallel it affords to many passages in the prophetical books of the Old Testament. It cannot, however, be too strongly insisted on that this similarity is purely external. Ipuwer is not an Egyptian Isaiah foretelling the wrath of God which is to come upon Israel and the form which it will take, but a mere mouthpiece for the author's stylistic eloquence. In other words this work was written not before but after the disasters which it describes. In so far as it is a prophecy it is a *post eventum* prophecy.

In connexion with it passing mention may be made of

the Complaint of Khakheperresenb, of which a fragment has come down to us on a pupil's writing-tablet now in the British Museum.[1] The passage preserved is the introduction, in which the speaker announces his desire to commune with his heart concerning the things that are happening in the land. No doubt the work was of the type so well known to us from other examples.

One passage, however, is of special interest. The writer says:

Would I had phrases that are not known, utterances that are strange, in new language that hath not been used, free from repetition; not an utterance that hath grown stale(?), which men of old have already spoken.

Here is a clue to the function of this type of literature. It is not prophecy, but a literary exercise. The subject of the distresses of the Early Intermediate Period was clearly a favourite with the writers of the Middle Kingdom, and their aim was to say something about it which had not been said before.

This is clearly shown by another work which obviously belongs to the same literary context, The Prophecies of Neferrohu, known to us from a papyrus in Leningrad.[2] Here the sage is represented as being summoned before King Sneferu of the IIIrd Dynasty in order to divert his majesty with words of wisdom. He foretells a period of confusion and foreign dominion.

Up, my heart, and bewail this land whence thou art sprung. Behold, that of which men spake as a thing to be dreaded now exists. Behold, the great one is fallen in the land whence thou art sprung. Be not thou weary, but rise up against what is before thee.

This land is ruined. None careth for it any more, none speaketh, none doeth. The sun is veiled and shineth not in the sight of men.

I will speak of what is before my face. I prophesy not something that is not yet come.

---

[1] Gardiner, *op. cit.*, pp. 95 ff. The name Khakheperresenb points to a XIIth-Dynasty date for the composition.

[2] *Journ. Eg. Arch.*, i, pp. 100 ff.

Gone, forsooth, are those good things of yore, the fish-ponds of them that slit [1] fish, teeming with fish and fowl. All good things are passed away. The land is fallen into misery by reason of that food of those Beduins who pervade the land. For foes are in the east, and Asiatics descend into Egypt. No protector hears.

The beasts of the desert shall drink from the streams of Egypt and take their ease on the sandbanks for lack of any to scare them away.

I show thee the land upside down, that which never happened before is come to pass. Men shall take weapons of warfare; the land lives in uproar. Men shall fashion arrows of copper; they crave for the bread of blood. Men laugh with the laughter of pain; there is none that weepeth because of death. None spendeth the night fasting because of death. A man's heart careth only for himself. No dishevelled locks are made to-day. A man sitteth in his corner careless, while one slayeth another. I show thee the son as an enemy, the brother as a foe, the man slaying his own father.

All good things have departed. Things done are as though they had never been done. A man's possessions are taken from him and given to him who is a stranger. I show the possessor as one in need, and the stranger as one who is sated.

Speech is in men's hearts as a fire. No utterance of the mouth is tolerated. The land is minished; its rulers are multiplied. He who was great of produce is destitute. Little is the corn, great the corn-measure; yet it is measured to overflowing. [2]

The Sun-god removes himself from men. If he shine it is but for an hour. None knoweth when midday comes, for his shadow is not discerned. The sight is not dazzled when he is beheld, the eyes are not moist with water. He is in the sky like the moon.

These excerpts show that we have here a very fine and powerful description of the state of things envisaged by the

---

[1] Large numbers of fish were slit open, cleaned, and dried in Egypt.
[2] Though corn is scanty the tithes are exacted in full measure.

poet, and the culmination of the whole, the withdrawal of the sun, is a poetic thought of great power and beauty.

But now mark the conclusion:

A king shall come from the south called Ameni, son of a woman of Nubia. The Asiatics shall fall before his carnage, and the Libyans shall fall before his flame. And there shall be built the Wall of the Ruler to prevent the Asiatics from going down into Egypt.

Now Ameni is a nickname for Amenemhet; and we know from the story of Sinuhe that the Wall of the Ruler was built by Amenemhet I, the first king of the XIIth Dynasty. It is therefore a fairly safe conjecture that this work was composed during or shortly after his reign, perhaps even by one who had himself gone through the dreadful times which he describes so vividly. Here, then, is no prophecy in the Old Testament sense, but an artificial literary form.

At the same time, though the original utterances of the Hebrew prophets must have been fundamentally different in form and purpose from the complaints of Ipuwer and Neferrohu, yet the Biblical books in which these utterances are preserved have much in common with the Egyptian compositions. This is due to the fact that the Books of the Prophets have come down to us not as mere collections of 'prophetic' oracles, but as literary compositions, often quite elaborate in form, in which these have been embodied and worked up.[1] The literary form thus given to them has brought about a formal resemblance to the Egyptian works which we must not allow to blind us to the essential underlying differences of origin and purpose.

We have now seen that the second branch of Egyptian wisdom-literature, namely the contemplative, or at any rate the more pessimistic form of this, had, if not an actual, at least a formal counterpart in the Old Testament. Babylonia, on the other hand, has not as yet contributed very much to this kind of writing. The works which most closely

---

[1] For a simple account of this process, see T. H. Robinson, *Prophecy and the Prophets* (London, 1925), Chap. V.

compare with those of Egypt and Palestine—and there are some—have precisely the same form as the more usual hymns and psalms. It has, however, been pointed out that, whatever their form, they must be regarded as purely literary productions which never had any connexion with the liturgy. For this reason they have been termed Literary Psalms.

The most famous of these is one which bore the title *I will praise the Lord of Wisdom*. The theme is that of the just man, here a king, who is at a loss to understand why the gods have sent him suffering, and the parallel with the book of Job is very striking. The text seems to have occupied four tablets, of which the third alone has survived, but a commentary on the poem, preserved on other tablets, enables portions of the first and second and possibly also the fourth to be reconstructed. Both text and commentary come from Assurbanipal's library, but the composition is clearly older than this date. Here are some excerpts: [1]

I have attained to long life, and passed even beyond it.
Wherever I turn me all is evil, yea evil;
My misery hath the upper hand of me, and I see not my happiness.
When I called to my god he vouchsafed not his countenance to me;
When I prayed to my goddess she lifted not up her head.
The seer by divination divined not the future;
By libation established he not my right.
When I had recourse to the oracle-monger he gave me no understanding,
Nor did the magician dissolve my ban by his magic.
What perverse things are everywhere!

If I looked behind me trouble followed,
As though I had made no libation to my god,
As though I had not summoned my goddess to the meal,
As though my face had not been downcast, and my prostration not seen.

[1] Weber, *Lit.*, p. 135.

As for me, I thought only upon prayer and supplication;
  Prayer was my rule, offering my custom.
The day of worship was my heart's delight;
  The day of following the goddess was profit and riches.
To worship the King [1] was my joy,
  And to pray to him my pleasure.
I taught my land to have heed to the name of God;
  I instructed my people to honour the name of the goddess.
The worship of the King made I mighty,
  And instructed the folk in reverence for the Palace.

O that I knew that such were well-pleasing to God!
Yet what seems good to oneself is evil in the sight of God,
  And what man despiseth is good in the sight of God.
Who shall understand the counsel of the gods in heaven?
  Who shall fathom the mysterious designs of God?
How shall dull men comprehend the way of a god?

He that was alive yestereven to-day is dead;
  Suddenly was he afflicted, quickly stricken down.
One moment he singeth and playeth,
  And the next he lamenteth like a mourner.
Men's mind changeth day and night.
When they are an hungered they are like a corpse,
  When they are filled they would rival their god.
When all is well with them they speak of mounting to heaven;
  When sorrow cometh they speak of descending to hell.

Another pessimistic work known to us from tablets of the ninth century B.C., but probably older in origin, is cast in a form which has no parallel either in Egyptian or in Hebrew literature.[2] It consists of dialogue between a master and his servant, in which the vanity of life is insisted on. The following stanza shows the form of the work:

'O servant, hearken unto me.' 'Yea, my lord, yea.'
'Hasten, order me water for my hands, give it to me and I will dine.'
'Dine, my lord, dine; to dine repeatedly is the opening of the heart;

---

[1] The god Bel?   [2] Langdon, *Babylonian Wisdom*, pp. 67 ff.

With him that dines in happiness and with washed hands shall
  Shamash walk.'
'Nay, O servant, I will not partake of the feast.'
'Thou shalt not dine, my lord, thou shalt not dine.'

In a series of stanzas of this kind the author seeks to
demonstrate the futility of seeking favour at court, of the
virtue of forgiveness, of the love of women, of worship of the
gods, of charity to neighbours. He concludes with the
reflection that both the benefactor and the malefactor
obtain the same reward, and that death is preferable to life.

'O my servant, hearken unto me.' 'Yea, my lord, yea.'
'A benefit unto my land will I do.' 'Do so, my lord, do so.
The man who doeth a benefaction unto his land
Findeth benefaction in the bowl of Marduk.'
'Nay, O servant, no benefaction unto my land will I do.'
'Do it not, my lord, do it not.
Ascend thou into the ruins of cities, go to those of old;
Behold the skulls of the latter and the former ones—
Which is now an evil doer, which now a benefactor ?'

'O servant, hearken unto me.' 'Yea, my lord, yea.'
'What then is good ?'
'To break my neck and thy neck,
To fall into the river is good.
Who is tall enough to ascend into heaven ?
Who is vast enough to complete the earth ?'
'Nay, O servant, I will slay thee and send thee before me.'
'O my lord, but three days shalt thou survive me.'

With these last two stanzas Langdon aptly compares
Ecclesiastes ix. 2 and Job iii. 20–2.
A third text which calls for notice is an acrostic and
alliterative poem of twenty-eight stanzas of eleven lines each
in which a sufferer complains of the injustice of both gods
and men.[1] It is a kind of Babylonian Koheleth. The

---

[1] Meissner, *Lit.*, p. 80 ; Jeremias, *Babylonische Dichtungen, Epen und
Legenden (Der Alte Orient,* Band 25), pp. 14–15.

sufferer was brought up in piety and godliness, but finds
that the old proverb 'He who serves the gods shall be happy'
does not apply in his case. The rich and the evil-doer alone
are fortunate, and consequently it is they who are wise.

The powerful man is wise and a possessor of discretion.
The heart of God is as far removed as the centre of heaven;
His might is felt in heaviness, yet men will not learn.
All the handiwork of the goddess Aruru [1] *is but a breath of air.*
The son of a prince is in all respects preferred.
The fool begets a son of renown;
  The strong and brave begets one whose name is altered.
So be it. Why should I bemoan, O God? Men will not be taught.
Heed then, my friend, give ear to my counsel,
  Guard the choice speech of my wisdom.
Men prize the word of the man of note who hath learnt to slay;
  Men belittle the weak who have no sin.
Men testify for the wicked to whom crime is righteousness;
  Men drive out the upright man, who seeks the advice of God.
Men give full measure of precious metal for him whose name is
    robber;
  Men plunder the income of him whose sustenance is scanty.
Men give power to the victorious whose gathering is crime;
  Men destroy the weak and smite the feeble.
Me too, enfeebled as I am, do the great ones persecute.

The poem ends with the reflection that for rich and poor
alike comes the 'secret of death'. The face grows pale, and
the journey over the river of the dead must be undertaken.
Even this certainty, however, does not affect the foolishness
of mankind, who continue to worship the idol of riches.
Curiously enough, in the last preserved lines we find the
sufferer actually praying to the very gods whom he has been
abusing.

The three works which we have just described show that
Babylonia had its counterpart to the pessimistic literature of
Egypt and Palestine. On the other hand, we found above

---

[1] A goddess who creates men.

that she has not as yet produced very much to set against the purely didactic works of the Egyptian writers, and if we take wisdom-literature as a whole we may fairly say that the contribution made by Egypt was the greater. Though the Hebrews probably owed much to both their predecessors, yet, on the evidence at present available, an impartial judge would probably maintain that they very much outshone their models in variety and originality of thought and expression. With such a judgement I have no quarrel. On the other hand, could the evidence in favour of Egyptian literature have been better prepared, that is to say, did we know Egyptian better than we do, had we accurate texts of its chief compositions instead of nearly unintelligible schoolboy copies, and had we at our disposal translators like those who produced the Authorized Version—then I believe that a different decision would have to be given, and it would have to be admitted that the Egyptian genius for this style of composition was just as lively as the Hebrew.

However this may be, the Hebrews did not emancipate wisdom-literature from the constraint and formality which Egypt and Babylonia had imprinted upon it, and in their hands it remained little more than collections of aphorisms. It was left for Montaigne with his *Essays* and Pascal with his *Pensées* to give to this type of literature the more flexible and cursive form which it has assumed in the modern world.[1]

Let us in conclusion try to sum up what Egypt accomplished for literature. Her greatest service may be stated in a single sentence: she was the first to cultivate literature for its own sake. As early as 2000 B.C. she was writing literary works which had no purpose whatsoever except to be literary works, which had no religious, political, or commercial interest. Her neighbours cannot question this

---

[1] The reduction of reflection to aphoristic form is the habit of a mind which is not essentially philosophic. Ptahhotep and Solomon reflected and produced proverbs; Plato reflected and produced the *Republic*. In other words, the Greeks were the world's first philosophers.

claim. Twelve hundred years later Hebrew literature was still in its cradle, and, though Babylonia may dispute with Egypt the priority of date, she can show little or no writing for writing's sake.

Now when we speak of literature for its own sake we pre-suppose two qualities, first form, and secondly style. Let us take them in this order. The forms used by the Egyptians were the lyric, the epic, and the didactic or reflective. That the first two arose in the country itself is very probable. Both are forms which have their roots in pre-writing litera-ture, and we may expect them to arise and to attain a certain development among any people which raises itself above the savage state. No doubt they arose in Babylonia in much the same way and at much the same date as in Egypt, and, even if it should ever be proved that the one was producing written examples earlier than the other, the possibility of independent origins in the two countries would still remain. At the same time it must be admitted that on present evidence Babylonia was a more fertile soil for the epic. There it grew up in the service of religion, and metrical forms were early applied to it. With the rich collection of epics which Sumeria and Babylonia produced, Egypt has little to compare, either because this type of literature never took a strong hold[1] there, or because the fate of survival has treated it unkindly. The latter is the more probable ex-planation, for the few epic fragments which remain, and the wealth of mythological allusion with which Egyptian litera-ture is filled, make it certain that the deeds of the gods at least were preserved in considerable detail throughout her history, even if in forms inferior, from the literary point of view, to those of Babylonia.

On the other hand, to the Egyptian must go the credit of having invented the short story as a literary form, and of having seen if not developed the possibilities of a psycho-logical treatment.

[1] It is significant that the New Kingdom schools seem to have ignored it.

In the field of lyric poetry both Egypt and Babylonia have much to their credit. In quantity Babylonia already leads the way, and, as excavation proceeds, she will increase her lead. So far as religious poetry is concerned there is little to choose in freshness and spontaneity between the best Babylonian work and that of the New Kingdom in Egypt, and if in the lyric field as a whole Egypt must be given first place it is because of her successful essays in profane lyric, an art which, so far as we know at present, was entirely neglected by the Babylonians. The best work of both was certainly equalled, perhaps even surpassed, by the Hebrews several centuries later. It remained for the Greeks, however, to outstrip their older neighbours, and by their genius to open up wholly undiscovered realms in lyric poetry, as indeed in every branch of literature.

The didactic or reflective form seems to have been the invention of the Egyptians. Once invented it appealed strongly to their taste, and the form persisted for centuries, undergoing, as the skill of the writers grew, a certain amount of development. We may not unreasonably speculate whether, but for the Proverbs of Ptahhotep, we should ever have had the Book of Proverbs and the Wisdom of Solomon. How did the ancient world get its belief in the wisdom of the Egyptians if it had never read their works?

Let us turn now to style. We have the evidence of the Egyptians themselves as to the esteem in which this was held. The Proverbs of Ptahhotep are called in one version *The beautifully expressed utterances* spoken by the vizier while instructing the ignorant in *knowledge and in the principles of elegant discourse.* King Sneferu in the Neferrohu papyrus commands his courtiers to summon for his diversion *one that will speak to me beautiful words, choice speeches, in hearing which my majesty may find diversion.* The Story of the Eloquent Peasant is but a framework for a series of set orations on the subject of justice. Here, then, is the world paying its first conscious tribute to eloquence. Here, before 2000 B.C., style is already an object in itself. Of this phenomenon there is no trace in Babylonia. Egypt was the first consciously literary nation in the world's history.

But style which is an end in itself carries with it a danger. Style should be fresh and natural, it should be adapted to the matter; indeed in the highest achievements of art it can hardly be disentangled from the matter, for the two are merged completely in each other. In Egypt, however, style soon outlived its first freshness, and gave way to an artificiality and bombast which submerge the content. These vices are already visible in the Middle Kingdom. They are not quite lacking in the Story of Sinuhe, and the speeches of the Eloquent Peasant are permeated by them. We know that the great works of this period were still being studied in the writing-schools of the New Empire, and that the exercises of the XIXth-Dynasty boy consisted in copying out the famous literary works of old, or in writing model letters whose style was an artificial imitation of that of the great age of literature. The atmosphere of the schools is well reflected by the curious document known as Papyrus Anastasi I,[1] a composition in the form of a satirical letter in which one scribe twits another with his ignorance not only of the art of letter-writing, but also of the means of calculating the weight of an obelisk and of the best methods of travelling in Syria. It is a dreary document, and, since it seems, from the number of partial copies extant, to have been a composition much used in the schools, one may hope, for the sake of the schoolboys, that it contained some kind of humour which is hidden from us.

The fact is that Egyptian literature, like Egyptian art, had passed its best before the New Empire, and that apart from an occasional outbreak of its pristine freshness and power it produced little of the highest merit. Lyric poetry offers an apparent exception to this statement. It may be that the prosperous light-hearted days of the XVIIIth and XIXth Dynasties found their expression in a spontaneous outburst

[1] A. H. Gardiner, *Pap. Anastasi I* (*Hieratic Literary Texts*, Leipzig, 1911).

of happy song; on the other hand it is possible that the loss of almost the whole of the lyric output of the Middle Kingdom has obscured for us the fact that much of what we deem best in the New Kingdom is of earlier origin.

Here then is another aspect of Egypt's achievement—she was the first to recognize style as an end in itself; and, if her too conscious striving after effect often caused her to miss the very goal at which she aimed, we must not refuse her the credit of having seen that there was such a goal.

It would be folly for me, who know neither Sumerian nor Babylonian, to discuss the question of style in the literature of Babylonia. I would say only this, that in it we find no conscious recognition of the value of style such as is the commonplace of Egyptian composition. I merely state this as a phenomenon, well aware that the most unconscious artist is often the best stylist.

We must not, however, lose our sense of proportion in appraising these early literatures. And we shall be little likely to do this if we ask ourselves how they compare with literature in the modern sense. A recent French literary critic has said,[1] 'There is no progress in literature. Tennyson is not greater than Homer, Proust is not greater than Montaigne, Strachey is not greater than Boswell. They are different. Literature follows a rhythmic beat rather than a continuous line.' Within the limits from which the writer's illustrations are taken the thesis is true. But when we go back beyond Homer it is false. It is precisely the interest of these ancient literatures, such as Egyptian and Babylonian, that they reveal to us the early stages in literature as such, and show us what a long and painful development was needed before the world could arrive at literature in the modern sense.

If we must define the points in which Egyptian and Babylonian literature fall short of the modern they are mainly three, first in their comparative lack of psychological interest, secondly in their very limited ability to produce

[1] André Maurois, *Aspects de la Biographie*, Paris, 1928, p. 177.

what is known as atmosphere, and thirdly in the complete absence of that magical conjuring with words which lies at the base of nearly everything which is greatest in literature.

Let us consider these in their order. The lack of psychological interest is of course most noticeable in Egyptian story-telling. Sinuhe has a mild psychological interest, in the sense that much of the story depends on the exile's longing for home and its fulfilment. But this is very simple and straightforward when compared with Henry James's *Daisy Miller* or Goethe's *Die Wahlverwandtschaften*. There is really little more psychology in Sinuhe than there is in Hans Andersen's fairy tales, and Gogol's *The Cloak* would have meant nothing to an Egyptian. But let us not blame the Egyptians for failing to produce a conception of story-telling which is purely modern.

Next we have to consider the question of atmosphere. It is a quality by which the reader is taken out of his own world into one of the author's creation, which is found vivid, interesting, convincing, and above all self-consistent. This is especially the work of drama, where the Babylonians and Egyptians made no serious essays. But it can also be a quality of epic and of lyric. Homer and Virgil have it, but I find little of it in Gilgamesh or Etana. All the best story-writing has it. Different writers get it in different ways, Balzac by the clumsy and yet strangely effective method of telling his reader every conceivable detail about all his characters and all his scenes. By the short-story writers it has to be done more subtly, and the best writers are those who do it with the fewest touches. Kipling and De Maupassant are masters of this art among the moderns. They work with strokes so delicate that the reader is unconscious of them as strokes and merely gets the general effect. This may be one of mystery, as in *They*, it may be one of horror, as in *Sur l'eau*; or it may be one so subtle that to define it would almost be to destroy it. The supreme example of this latter type in English is perhaps Coleridge's *Ancient Mariner*.

Now there are just two works from Ancient Egypt which seem to have a trace of this literary quality. They are the stories of Sinuhe and Wenamun. Neither produces the quantity or quality of atmosphere produced by the best modern stories, but both achieve something in this direction. Sinuhe and Wenamun both take us to Syria with them. Their Syria is real, and they make us see it as they saw it. The strokes by which they do this are often very evident, but they are not ineffective. The presence of this quality in these two stories will be well realized if they be compared with such others as the tales of the Westcar Papyrus, The Foredoomed Prince, and The Two Brothers. Here are stories well and simply told, but nothing more. These are milk for babes. Sinuhe and Wenamun are food for men; they are the earliest good short stories in the world, and as such they are a contribution to literature.

And finally we come to the third literary quality which the Babylonians and Egyptians lacked, namely, what I have called the power of conjuring with words. On the existence of this quality nearly the whole value of modern literature is based. The power 'out of three sounds' to 'form not a fourth sound but a star' is not, as Abt Vogler thought it might be, confined to music, it is just as true of literature. Here, however, the magician has not mere sounds to juggle with, for his sounds make words, and words have meaning. No philosophy of aesthetics can analyse to the end the qualities which make Keats's *Ode to a Nightingale* a sublime work of art. Subtract the first element, the lofty imaginative power, and it can only be said that the rest lies in the use of the particular words chosen and no others. Shakespeare in the midst of a prose passage in a comedy can take our breath away with the lines:

DON PEDRO. *Runs not this speech like iron through your blood?*
CLAUDIO. *I have drunk poison whiles he utter'd it.*

and in just twenty-four words he can resolve the tragedy of Lear and make it tolerable:

Vex not his ghost: O! let him pass; he hates him
That would upon the rack of this tough world
Stretch him out longer.[1]

This is what the moderns can do with words. It is to this power that we must attribute that 'atmosphere of infinite suggestion' which Professor A. C. Bradley says 'floats about the best poetry. The poet speaks to us of one thing, but in this one thing there seems to lurk the secret of all.'

Could the Egyptian or the Babylonian[2] do this with words? The answer must be No. The art of conjuring with words in the modern sense was the discovery of the Greeks, in the first place of Homer, and, in a still more developed sense, of the tragedians and lyric poets. Egyptian was a language which, despite a certain aridity, was not devoid of metaphor; indeed we know that however far back we go in the known languages of civilized peoples language is a mass of metaphor. Egyptian poets knew, too, the value of simile, and made use of it in their work; yet such word-painting as κυμάτων ἀνήριθμον γέλασμα, 'consuming the last clouds of cold mortality,' or 'the gold gateways of the stars' lay far beyond the boundaries of their art. The Hebrews with their lofty imagination and their love of simile went further in the domain of poetic diction, but the sublime art of which I speak, the art which makes literature what it is, was reserved for the Greeks.

We shall realize what the absence of this quality means if we compare the Egyptian and the modern treatments of the same or a similar subject. In the *Dialogue of a Man with his Soul*, perhaps the most poetical of all Egyptian works, we

---

[1] Sophocles produces an exactly parallel effect in *Oed. Col.*, ll. 1658–65.

[2] The reader may not unreasonably wonder whether one who does not know Babylonian is in a position to judge of this point. I reply that the quality in question is one which cannot fail to show itself to some extent even in translation. The translators of Babylonian literature would hardly have suppressed so effectively a quality whose existence they would have been only too anxious to emphasize.

have a short lyric in praise of death (see above, pp. 116-17).
It begins:

> *Death is in my eyes today*
> *As when a sick man becomes whole,*
> *As the walking abroad after illness.*

This poem contains a number of well conceived similes,
and has considerable aesthetic value. But compare it with
what the moderns have said of death, with Hamlet's great
soliloquy, with Shelley's *Adonais*, with Keats's *Ode to a
Nightingale*, with 'fair-haired Milton's eloquent distress'—
and it sinks into insignificance. And it does so not so much
because these are superior in imaginative power, although
that is part of the reason, but because they are infinitely
superior in the art of using words:

> *For many a time*
> *I have been half in love with easeful Death,*
> *Called him soft names in many a mused rhyme,*
> *To take into the air my quiet breath;*
> *Now more than ever seems it rich to die,*
> *To cease upon the midnight with no pain,*
> *While thou art pouring forth thy soul abroad*
> *In such an ecstasy.*

There is more poetry in each line of this than in the whole
of the Egyptian lyric.

I have insisted on the inferiority of Egyptian literature to
modern not in order to belittle the Egyptians, for the purpose
of my lectures is to show their greatness, but because I wish
it to be quite clear exactly how much I claim for them. In
the history of early literature they occupy a position of
immense importance. As early as 2000 B.C. they had a
national literature of a high order, for which they were
indebted probably to no outside influence. This literature
seems to have run to seed in later times, and it was left for
a greater nation, the Greeks, to make the advances in conception which alone made literature in the modern sense

possible. At the same time, Greek literature cannot have sprung full-grown like Venus from the waves, any more than did Greek art, and though we may never learn the manner in which Egyptian influence made its way into Hebrew and into Greek literature, it may reasonably be doubted whether either the one or the other would have been what it is had it not been for Egypt.